AUNT OLA

AFRICAN AMERICAN PEOPLE and NATIVE AMERICAN INDIAN TRIBES

Compiled and edited by
Eleyes Y. Reeves
BA, BFA, LAT

AUNT OLA
AFRICAN AMERICAN PEOPLE and NATIVE AMERICAN INDIAN TRIBES

Compiled and edited by
Eleyes Y. Reeves
BA, BFA, LAT

Warrior Angel Publishing
Indianapolis

Warrior Angel Publishing
Indianapolis, Indiana

© 2024 Eleyes Y. Reeves

All Rights Reserved. No part of this book may be reproduced in any manner whatsoever without the written permission of the author, except for brief quotations embodied in critical articles, reviews and writings on related subjects.

First Edition 2024

ISBN:

Cover Design by James C. Anyike and Eleyes Y. Reeves

Printed in the United States of America

DEDICATED TO

Jesus Christ, Son of The Living God

Table of Content

Introduction	1
Larry Sellers – No.2	3
Nayenezgani – No.4	3
Inuit People	3
Chief Black Hair and Daughter – No.7	4
Black Eagle, The Nez Perce – No.6	4
Three Apache Brothers 1880 – No.8	4
Black Shawl 1888	4
Chief Crazy Horse	5
The Hunkpapa Lakota Group – No.36	5
Kaw-U-Tz , Model a Caddo Nation member – No.38	5
Quanah Parker and his two wives Topay and Chonie	6
Cynthia Ann Parker – No.10	6
Bear Bull	7
Yellow Tail	7
Geronimo's daughter Lenna – No.108	7
Choctaw	7
Mescalero Apache	9
Keanu Reeves	9
Chief Dan George Actor (Story) – No.3	10
Gertrude Three Finger – No.1	13
Cynthia Ann Parker – No.10	13
Muscogee Will (Sonny) Sampson Actor – No.11	13
The Piegan	14
The Arapaho	15
Chief John Smith – No.14	15
Brown Weasel Woman	15
Elsie Vance Chestnen – No.15	17
Tatanka Means	18
Chief Big Tree - No.16	18
Black Eagle – No.17	19

Sioux Chief Long Wolf & Family 1880 – No.18	19
Flying Hawk – No.19	20
Shosone Warrior Gor-osimp – No.71	22
Cher (Cherilyn Sarkisian)	22
Dust Maker (Pete Mitchell)	22
Chief Blue Horse	23
Chief Dull Knife	23
Wanada Parker Page – No.47	24
Steve Reevis	24
Flying Hawk – No.78	25
Dewey Beard or Wasa Masa	26
Cheyenne Dog Soldiers	26
Crazy Horse – No.58	26
Wes Studi (actor)	27
Two Leggins - stories	28
Chief Joseph Medicine Crow – No.106	29
Rodney A. Grant	29
Cherokee	29
Nez Perce Black Eagle – No.6	31
Sarah Rector (millionaire)	31
The Kiowa	32
Chief Two Moons – No.26	34
Brenda Schad (Model) – No.20	35
Chief Running Antelope – No.28	35
Mary Frances Thompson Fisher – No.30	36
The Quechan or Yuma	37
Chief Red Fish – No.32	37
Sarah Winnemucca 1880 – No.33	38
Quanah Parker and his two wives Topay & Chonie – No.41	41
Cynthia Ann Parker – No.10	41
White Buffalo	41
Chief Crowfoot	42
Jay Silverheels – No.43	43
Nampeyo – No.44	43

Chief Dan George Actor – No.3	44
Walker Calhoun	44
Ute Pass Trail	44
The Dekota Nation	45
Crazy Horse	45
Ute warrior tribe – No.59	45
Ramona Dak Lugie 1898	46
Nanye-Hi (Nancy Ward) – No.76	47
Brushing Against – No.64	48
Chief Buffalo Sundown – No.65	48
White Buffalo – No.66 and 67	49
Floyd Red Crow Westerman – No.69	49
Indiana Marriage Story (Comanche)	50
The Human & The Bison – No.70	51
The Sacred Bear (Story)	53
A large Black Family in one little house – No.73	56
Curley Scout for General Custer	56
Henry Oscar One Bull – No.75	57
Chief Two Guns White Calf – No.77	57
Native Encampment (Story)	58
Story by Flying Hawk – No.78	59
Geraldine Keams	60
Rose Bompard Bird – No.81	61
Standing Bear – No.83	61
Chief Blue Horse – No.84	62
Indiana poem (poet unknown)	63
Medicine Crow and son – No.89	63
Yakama Woman – No.88	63
Chief Iron Tail	63
Hash-Nash-Shut – No.91	66
Trade Blankets	67
Bull Chief – No.92	67
Iron Eagle (Indian Story)	69
The Cherokee Kid	71

Death in the Tribe (Three Generations-Alfredo Rodriguez 1954)	71
Dog Travois (elk dogs or big dogs)	72
Chief Thunderhawk – No.95	72
C.E. Herman Ase Nap	72
Comanche Elder Post Oak Jim (Tahkahper)	73
Fast Thunder	73
William Bald Eagle (actor)	74
Omaha Dance	74
Cheyenne Sun Dance	75
The Grass Dance	75
Ghost Dance Movement ends	75
Chief Big Foot	75
Mary Louise Defender Wilson (Indian storyteller)	76
White Buffalo – No.66	77
Chief American Horse (Story) – No.102	78
Moving Robe Woman – No.103	78
A little Pikuni (Blackfeet) boy with wool leggings – No.104	79
Medicine Crow – No.106	79
Thate Iyohiwig – No.105	81
Zitkala-Sa	81
Buffalo Calf Road Woman – No.107	83
Fool Thunder and family Hunkpapa Lakota	83
Comanche Little Chief – No.111	86
Rain-In-the -Face - No 114	87
Member of the Dreaded Cheyenne dog Soldiers	88
The Story of the Buffalo Dance (A Blackfoot Legend)	88
Bill Pickett – No.61	92
Cochise – No.62	93
Comanche Chief Quanah Parker – No.39	94
The Cheyenne Warrior Red Blanket – No.49	94
Mildred Imoch Cleghorn – No.21	94
A member of the Miami Tribe – No.115	95
Lame White Man	95
Yellow Wolf – No.99	96

Red Cloud – No.24 and 51   96
Chief Sitting Bull – No.50   97

Picture Collection   99
About the Author   135

Introduction

This book is dedicated to Jesus Christ Son of the Living God. This book was created because of the question of what happen? Why and how did my Great-grandmother leave the Cheyenne Reservation? I don't know if she was married with children or when she left the reservation who helped her or what was her Indian name when she departed? Who was she married to while on the reservation? When did she travel to Indiana? Why did she come here to Indiana to make her home and raise her family? I know she ended up marrying a Black man and she had daughters and one of those daughters was my grandmother Rachel Augusta (Gussie) (Hunt) Holiday and she (Gussie) married John Holiday and they had several children and one of them the baby of the family was my mother Betty Jean (Holiday) Reeves. My mother told me about her grandmother how she was so beautiful and that her husband stayed behind at the reservation but she left in a wagon and saw President Lincoln. Then my cousin gave a picture of her to my sister of the great-grandmother and my sister gave me a copy of the great grandmother she was so beautiful, but my mother had died and never saw this but my father, Richard Alaska Reeves Sr. was living, and he said it was her because he met her and talked to her.

Mrs. Britt Sutton of ArtMix was telling me about her beautiful grandmother who had died, her Indian name was Chipeta and she was of the Ute tribe. Ms. Britt went to the Ute reservation and found her grandmother's brother, Ms. Britt's grandmother Chipeta had been taken from her family at 4 or 5 years old and placed in a mission she never saw her mother or father again. I never got to meet my Great grandmother only through my mother talking about her and I did get to meet my great grandmother's daughter Aunt Ola. She was the first and only link that I saw that we were totally connected to the Cheyenne tribe. Aunt Ola had one child a son who had several children and he lived with them in Ohio. My mother loved Aunt Ola and her son very much because they kept the traditions and customs of the Cheyenne tribe alive in my family. Aunt Ola had authentic headdresses, the clothing, trade blankets, a teepee and Aunt Ola spoked the language. Aunt Ola, her mother and all her sisters went to the same church Scott United Methodist Church on 22nd And Dr Andrew J Brown Avenue (it is still standing today) but then it was Martindale. After Aunt Ola died, I never saw the Cheyenne clothing, headdresses, or the teepee again I never saw her son or any of his children again either, they were disconnected from me. This book has restored the disconnections for me and hopefully it will help find someone's Indian heritage link if you are African American.

As I was gathering the information on the great Indians from the various nations and I suddenly realized that was her, that was my great grandmother, the photograph was identical to my photograph. The Cheyenne maiden's name was Gertrude Three Finger and now I understood that once you leave the reservation you lose your identity and your name is no longer Indian, you can't speak your language, wear any of your Indian clothing, your braids are discontinued or cut, and you have been declared not Native American Indian anymore but that's not the case today. A lot of people especially children were subjected to this. So, I had a picture of my niece (Raven Simone Reeves) and she looks just like the great grandmother Gertrude Three Finger and I said this is her as a young woman Wow! This is what happened.

This book is a composition reference book of Anecdotes accumulated to form the necessary history that was lost. It is a series of traditional stories carried down from generation to generation allowing the reader to become a part of the Native American way of life, their purpose, their family spiritual and physical. With this positive pictorial item, the reader is able to better connect to the tribe while connecting their relatives to Black people today.

By Eleyes Y. Reeves, BA BFA LAT

Anecdotes

Larry Sellers (1949–2021), Lakota and Cherokee, best known for "Dr. Quinn Medicine Woman." RNCI Board member from 1995 – 2021. Larry served on our RNCI Board of Directors since the beginning and most recently moved to serve on RNCI Advisory Board. He was a Sun dancer and Chanunpa carrier.'Joanelle Romero. Osage, Cherokee, and Lakota. Traditional ceremonial leader, actor and stuntman who played the leading Indian role Cloud Dancing (for which he received an Emmy nomination for Best Supporting Actor) in the popular series "Dr. Quinn, Medicine Woman". While on Dr. Quinn, Sellers is credited as the show's Native American Consultant.

A Navajo tribe member wears a **Nayenezgani**, a ceremonial garment 1903. The Navajo tribe had deeply rooted traditions that they held precious. The most important one was the Nayenezgani, translated to "slayer of alien gods." They believe that the Nayenezgani protected the tribe from evil spirits who were among them on Earth. Navajo legends state that the Nayenezgani works together with his twin brother, Tobadzischini, to kill these evil spirits and turning them into stone. The stone structures are what make the huge rock formation labeled today as Monument Valley, Arizona. The Navajo tribe still wear their masks to showcase the monster killer in the ceremonies they performed.

The **Inuit people** can't be imagined without their signature **parkas**, fashioned from fur and hide of the local wildlife. One of the many reasons why early European voyages into the Arctic circle failed is because they were underprepared for the extreme weather conditions of the north. They wore wool clothing, which kept them hot on the inside, but made them sweat a lot, which made their clothing freeze in the extreme temperatures. The Inuit never faced this problem, as they have been making their parkas from caribou deer or seal hide from as early as 22,000 BC (Siberia). The production of these parkas took weeks, and the tradition of making them was passed down from mother to daughter, taking years to master. Depending on the geographical location of the tribes, the design of the parkas varied according to the types of animals available. Beadwork, fringes and pendants frequently decorated the clothing. Roald Amundsen was the first explorer who outfitted his crew with Inuit clothing, which enabled him to successfully circumvent the North-West Passage in 1906. In the 20th century the use of traditional Inuit clothing declined, but it has seen a recent resurgence, as the Inuit strive to preserve their culture. See **Chief Black Hair and daughter**, circa 1900; the Crow (Apsáalooke) Chief (1849-1905) posed with Mary Black Hair (1896-1953) in the Black Lodge District of the Crow Reservation in Eastern Montana; the Chief's eagle feather fan and numerous ermine danglers indicated a person of standing; and Mary's dress was adorned with elk ivories (elk have two teeth made of ivory).

Photographer Fred E. Miller had married a Native woman and was adopted into the Crow tribe in 1905. His photographs gained recognition with the 1985 publication of "Fred E. Miller: Photographer of the Crows."

The Nez Perce, Black Eagle must have been the rock star of his time. Edward Curtis/ Courtesy~Portland Art Museum.

In New Spain of the latter 1600's, **the Utes** had the ability to capture and maintain horses. Their horses allowed for movement and hunting over much greater distances. Around the same time, other Numic speaking people historically known as Comanches soon moved onto the landscape of the Great Plains.

Black Shawl fellow tribesmen - the Spanish authorities noted the evergrowing power of the Utes and their Comanche allies. It was also noticed that the raiders from the North had extreme confidence in their abilities to raid communities. The Comanches and the Utes battled for control of the land and soon expanded their territory.

In the early 1700's, the brethren tribes fought for excellent raiding and trading sites along the Rio Grande River. As both the Apache and Navajo were driven out, they sought help and protection from the Spanish. Over time, the Comanches had come to control the rich grasslands of the Southern Plains and the powerful Utes towered over northwestern New Mexico.

In the 1740's, traders in Navajo country observed that Navajos had to "live on the top of the mesas in little houses of stone. And that the reason for their living in those mountains is because the Yutas and Comanches make war upon them."

See the impressive historical picture of the known Yamparika Comanche Chief Howea (Gap in the Woods) by William S. Soule, Fort Sill, circa 1872. Howea is shown wearing a shirt and a patterned vest. Courtesy of the Wilbur S. Nye Collection.

Black Shawl (1888) was known as the wife of **Crazy Horse**. **Crazy Horse** was one of the most notorious Native Americans of the 19th century. He was a Lakota war leader who fought against the US to keep his tribe's land from being turned over to the government.

He married Black Shawl after his battle, before that he was with a woman named Black Buffalo Woman, who was married to No Water. When No Water found out, he shot Crazy Horse in the jaw. Black Shawl was then sent to help him and nurse him to good health. She was of the Oglala Lakota, and they fell in love instantly. The two were married in 1871 and had a daughter.

The Washoe Tribe originally lived around Lake Tahoe and adjacent areas of the Great Basin. Their tribe's name derives from the Washoe word, waashiw (wa·šiw), meaning "people from here." See photo: Washoe Indians, Lake Tahoe, 1866, Lawrence and Houseworth African features.

Dance has always been able to remind me of who I am. And that is a Native American.' — Kenneth Shirley of the Diné (Navajo) and his intertribal dance troupe are bringing Indigenous dance culture to the world Video.

Kaw-Utz, a Caddo Nation members spread out through the parts of Oklahoma, Arkansas, Louisiana, and Texas. The tribe dealt mainly in farming and did not like outsiders. Their farming skills were unparalleled, as they were able to grow squash, beans, and corn in areas that were humid swamps. The Caddo typically lived in grass huts in the shape of a cone.

Historians believe that they were kind to the Spanish explorers who arrived in the area because they were given many compliments about how they furnished their homes. The Caddo people also use the areas pine trees to make their famed bow and arrows.

The Crow are also called the Apsáalooke, Absaroka, and Apsaroke. Their name was given them by the Hidatsa, and meant "people [or children] of the large-beaked bird." Historically, they lived in the Yellowstone River Valley. A Siouan tribe, they once were part of the Hidatsa, living around the headwaters of the upper Mississippi River in northern Minnesota and Wisconsin. Later, the Crow moved to the Devil's Lake region of North Dakota, before splitting with the Hidatsa and moving westward.

Settling in Montana, the tribe split once again into two divisions, called the Mountain Crow and the River Crow. They were first encountered by two

Frenchmen in 1743 near the present-day town of Hardin, Montana. When the Lewis and Clark expedition came upon them in 1804, they estimated some 350 lodges with about 3,500 members.

See picture of **Quanah Parker and two of his wives, Topay and Chonie.** **Quanah Parker** was the last Chief of the Comanches and never lost a battle to the white man. His tribe roamed over the area where Pampas stands. He was never captured by the army, but decided to surrender and lead his tribe into the white man's culture, only when he saw that there was no alternative. His was the last tribe in the Staked Plains to come into the reservation system. **Quanah**, meaning "fragrant," was born about 1850, son of Comanche Chief Peta Nocona and Cynthia Ann Parker, a white girl taken captive during the 1836 raid on Parker's Fort, Texas.

Cynthia Ann Parker was recaptured, along with her daughter, during an 1860 raid on the Pease River in northwest Texas. She had spent 24 years among the Comanche, however, and thus never readjusted to living with the whites again.

She died in Anderson County, Texas, in 1864 shortly after the death of her daughter, Prairie Flower. Ironically, Cynthia Ann's son would adjust remarkably well to living among the white men. But first he would lead a bloody war against them.

Quanah and the Quahada Comanche, of whom his father, Peta Nocona had been chief, refused to accept the provisions of the 1867 Treaty of Medicine Lodge, which confined the southern Plains Indians to a reservation, promising to clothe the Indians and turn them into farmers in imitation of the white settlers.

Knowing of past lies and deceptive treaties of the "White man", Quanah decided to remain on the warpath, raiding in Texas and Mexico and out maneuvering Army Colonel Ronald S. Mackenzie and others. He was almost killed during the attack on buffalo hunters at Adobe Walls in the Texas Panhandle in 1874. The U.S. Army was relentless in its Red River campaign of 1874-75. Quanah's allies, the Quahada were weary and starving.

Mackenzie sent Jacob J. Sturm, a physician and post interpreter, to solicit the Quahada's surrender. Sturm found Quanah, whom he called "a young man of much influence with his people," and pleaded his case. Quanah rode to a mesa, where he saw a wolf come toward him, howl and trot away to the northeast. Overhead, an eagle "glided lazily and then whipped his wings in the direction of Fort Sill," in the words of Jacob Sturm. This was a sign, Quanah thought, and on June 2, 1875, he and his band surrendered at Fort Sill in present-day Oklahoma.

RETURNING HOME TO THE STRONGHOLD: Except for Plains Apache; Lipan, Jicarilla, Coyotero, and Kiowa, they are a mountain people. Once they retreated to the stronghold, pursuing them took a lot of work and was extremely hazardous. Masters of concealment, they could be 6-8 feet away, and the enemy would never sense it.

Bear Bull, Siksika (Northern Blackfoot of Canada) elder, 1926. Bear Bull had a tightly woven topknot of braided hair above the forehead, which indicated he was a keeper of a Thunder Medicine Pipe bundle. Clay dust gave a lighter color to his hair below the topknot. I regularly post my restorations of Old West photos, and the stunning side-profile portrait grabbed my notice. The Siksika Nation is in Alberta, Canada.

Photographer Edward S. Curtis published "The North American Indian," a 20-volume work that took 23 years to complete. It contained 1,500 photographs, a forward by President Teddy Roosevelt, and the first written history for several tribes.

See **Yellow Tail**, (Hawk with Yellow Tail Feathers), rare and magnificent hand-colored portrait, likely 1905-11. He wore a porcupine hair roach. He was father to Robert Yellowtail, who became an important leader of Montana's Crow (Apsáalooke).

At age 13, Robert Yellowtail was sent to California's Sherman Institute, graduating from the high school at age 17. In 1910, Chief Plenty Coup asked Robert, age 21, to return home and help fight against efforts to open the Reservation to White homesteaders. In 1934, Yellowtail was appointed as Agency Superintendent, the first Native to hold the post.

See the **Geronimo daughter Lenna** photo ca.1900. Lenna was born in 1886 in Fort Marion, St.Augustine, Fl, while her father was prisoner there. The Medical staff gave her the name Marion, after the fort, but she took back the name Lenna when returning to the South-West. Lenna Geronimo, the daughter of Geronimo and Ih-tedda, a Mescalero Apache, was the full sister of Robert Geronimo, Geronimo only living.

The **Choctaw Tribe** (Dark skinned African featured Indians) were first noted by Europeans in French written records of 1675. Their mother mound is Nanih Waiya, a great earthwork platform mound located in central-east Mississippi. Early Spanish explorers of the mid-16th century in the Southeast encountered ancestral Mississippian culture villages and chiefs.

The Choctaw coalesced as a people in the 17th century and developed at least three distinct political and geographical divisions: eastern, western, and southern. These different groups sometimes created distinct, independent alliances with nearby European powers. These included the French, based on the Gulf Coast and in Louisiana; the English of the Southeast, and the Spanish of Florida and Louisiana during the colonial era.

Most Choctaw allied with the Americans during American Revolution, War of 1812, and the Red Stick War, most notably at the Battle of New Orleans. European Americans considered the Choctaw to be one of the "Five Civilized Tribes" of the Southeast. The Choctaw and the United States agreed to a total of nine treaties. By the last three, the US gained vast land cessions in the Southeast. As part of Indian Removal, despite not having waged war against the United States, the majority of Choctaw were forcibly relocated to Indian Territory from 1831 to 1833. The Choctaw government in Indian Territory had three districts, each with its own chief, who together with the town chiefs sat on their National Council.

Those Choctaw who chose to stay in the state of Mississippi were considered state and U.S. citizens; they were one of the first major nonEuropean ethnic groups to be granted citizenship. Article 14 in the 1830 treaty with the Choctaw stated Choctaws may wish to become citizens of the United States under the 14th Article of the Treaty of Dancing Rabbit Creek on all of the combined lands which were consolidated under Article I from all previous treaties between the United States and the Choctaw.

During the American Civil War, the Choctaw in both Indian Territory and Mississippi mostly sided with the Confederate States of America. Under the late 19th-century Dawes Act and Curtis Acts, the US federal government broke up tribal land holdings and dissolved tribal governments in Indian Territory in order to extinguish Indian land claims before admission of Oklahoma as a state in 1907. From that period, for several decades the US Bureau of Indian Affairs appointed chiefs of the Choctaw and other tribes in the former Indian Territory.

During World War I, Choctaw soldiers served in the US military as some of the first Native American code talkers, using the Choctaw language.

Since the Indian Reorganization Act of 1934, the Choctaw people in three areas have reconstituted their governments and gained federal recognition. The largest are the Choctaw Nation in Oklahoma.

Since the 20th century, the Mississippi Band of Choctaw Indians were federally recognized in 1945, the Choctaw Nation of Oklahoma in 1971, and the Jena Band of Choctaw Indians in 1995.

Two Young Mescalero Apache men, 1888 - The Mescalero Apaches were a semi-nomadic people who once roamed the area of New Mexico, West Texas, and Chihuahua. The word "Apache" means "enemy" in the Zuñi language, as they were feared by the pueblo tribes of northern New Mexico as well by the Spanish. The Gila and Chiricahua Apaches were to the west and the Lipan Apaches to the east, but the Mescaleros were once the largest and most powerful Apache nation among them.

The Mescaleros are documented archeologically in our region as early as the thirteenth century. They began raiding local Spanish settlements and traveling caravans starting in the 1680s. Between 1778 and 1825 there was a large band of Mescaleros encamped on the future site of Duranguito and Downtown El Paso, peaking at about one thousand men, women and children in the 1790s.

The Spanish, Mexicans and Americans all waged wars of extermination against this proud and fierce people. Today the remaining Mescaleros possess a small reservation in southern New Mexico.Credit: Photo by A. Frank Randall, Smithsonian, NAA: 2491-a.

Keanu Reeves was abandoned by his father at 3 years old and grew up with 3 different stepfathers. He is dyslexic. His dream of becoming a hockey player was shattered by a serious accident. His daughter died at birth. His wife died in a car accident. His best friend, River Phoenix, died of an overdose. His sister has leukemia.

And with everything that has happened, Keanu Reeves never misses an opportunity to help people in need. When he was filming the movie "The Lake House," he overheard the conversation of two costume assistants; One cried because he would lose his house if he did not pay $20,000 and on the same day Keanu deposited the necessary amount in the woman's bank account; He also donated stratospheric sums to hospitals.

In 2010, on his birthday, Keanu walked into a bakery and bought a brioche with a single candle, ate it in front of the bakery, and offered coffee to people who stopped to talk to him. After winning astronomical sums for the Matrix trilogy, the actor donated more than $50 million to the staff who handled the costumes and special effects - the true heroes of the trilogy, as he called them. He also gave a Harley-Davidson to each of the stunt doubles. A total expense of several million dollars. And for many successful films, he has even given up 90% of his salary to allow the production to hire other stars. In 1997 some paparazzi found him walking one morning in the company of a homeless man in Los Angeles, listening to him and sharing his life for a few hours. Most stars when they make a charitable gesture they declare it to all the media. He has never claimed to be doing charity, he simply does it as a matter of moral principles and not to look better in the eyes of others.

This man could buy everything, and instead every day he gets up and chooses one thing that cannot be bought: To be a good person. Keanu Reeves' father is of Native Hawaiian descent.

> *This is written by **Chief Dan George**, "In the course of my life time I have lived in two distinct cultures. I was born into a culture that lived in communal houses. My grandfather's house was eighty feet long. It was called a smoke house, and it stood down by the beach along the inlet. All my grandfather's sons and their families lived in this dwelling. Their sleeping apartments were separated by blankets made of bull rush weeds, but one open fire in the middle served the cooking needs of all. In houses like these, throughout the tribe, people learned to live with one another; learned to respect the rights of one another. And children shared the thoughts of the adult world and found themselves surrounded by aunts and uncles and cousins who loved them and did not threaten them. My father was born in such a house and learned from infancy how to love people and be at home with them.*
>
> *And beyond this acceptance of one another there was a deep respect for everything in nature that surrounded them. My father loved the earth and all its creatures. The earth was his second mother. The earth and everything it contained was a gift from See-see-am...and the way to thank this great spirit was to use his gifts with respect.*
>
> *I remember, as a little boy, fishing with him up Indian River and I can still see him as the sun rose above the mountain top in the early morning...I can see him standing by the water's edge with his arms*

raised above his head while he softly moaned... 'Thank you, thank you.' It left a deep impression on my young mind.

And I shall never forget his disappointment when once he caught me gaffing for fish 'just for the fun of it.' 'My son' he said, 'The Great Spirit gave you those fish to be your brothers, to feed you when you are hungry. You must respect them. You must not kill them just for the fun of it.'

This then was the culture I was born into and for some years the only one I really knew or tasted. This is why I find it hard to accept many of the things I see around me.

I see people living in smoke houses hundreds of times bigger than the one I knew. But the people in one apartment do not even know the people in the next and care less about them.

It is also difficult for me to understand the deep hate that exists among people. It is hard to understand a culture that justifies the killing of millions in past wars, and it at this very moment preparing bombs to kill even greater numbers. It is hard for me to understand a culture that spends more on wars and weapons to kill, than it does on education and welfare to help and develop.

It is hard for me to understand a culture that not only hates and fights his brothers but even attacks nature and abuses her.

I see my white brothers going about blotting out nature from his cities. I see him strip the hills bare, leaving ugly wounds on the face of mountains. I see him tearing things from the bosom of mother earth as though she were a monster, who refused to share her treasures with him. I see him throw poison in the waters, indifferent to the life he kills there; and he chokes the air with deadly fumes.

My white brother does many things well for he is more clever than my people but I wonder if he has ever really learned to love at all. Perhaps he only loves the things that are outside and beyond him. And this is, of course, not love at all, for man must love all creation or he will love none of it. Man must love fully or he will become the lowest of the animals. It is the power to love that makes him the greatest of them all...for he alone of all animals is capable of love. Love is something you and I must have. We must have it because our spirit feeds upon it. We must have it because without it we become weak and faint. Without love our self esteem weakens. Without it our courage fails. Without love we can no longer look out confidently at the world. Instead we turn inwardly and begin to feed upon our own personalities and little by little we destroy ourselves.

You and I need the strength and joy that comes from knowing that we are loved. With it we are creative. With it we march tirelessly. With it, and with it alone, we are able to sacrifice for others.

There have been times when we all wanted so desperately to feel a reassuring hand upon us...there have been lonely times when we so wanted a strong arm around us...I cannot tell you how deeply I miss my wife's presence when I return from a trip. Her love was my greatest joy, my strength, my greatest blessing.

I am afraid my culture has little to offer yours. But my culture did prize friendship and companionship. It did not look on privacy as a thing to be clung to, for privacy builds walls and walls promote distrust. My culture lived in a big family community, and from infancy people learned to live with others.

My culture did not prize the hoarding of private possessions, in fact, to hoard was a shameful thing to do among my people. The Indian looked on all things in nature as belonging to him and he expected to share them with others and to take only what he needed.

Everyone likes to give as well as receive. No one wishes only to receive all the time. We have taken something from your culture...I wish you had taken something from our culture...for there were some beautiful and good things in it.

Soon it will be too late to know my culture, for integration is upon us and soon we will have no values but yours. Already many of our young people have forgotten the old ways. And many have been shamed of their Indian ways by scorn and ridicule. My culture is like a wounded deer that has crawled away into the forest to bleed and die alone.

The only thing that can truly help us is genuine love. You must truly love, be patient with us and share with us. And we must love you— with a genuine love that forgives and forgets...a love that gives the terrible sufferings your culture brought ours when it swept over us like a wave crashing along a beach...with a love that forgets and lifts up its head and sees in your eyes an answering love of trust and acceptance.

This is brotherhood...anything less is not worthy of the name.

I have spoken.

Gertrude Three Finger, was a Cheyenne tribe member (1892). William E. Irwin was a photographer who worked across Arizona, New Mexico, and Oklahoma during the 19th and 20th centuries. He captured several photos of Southwestern Native Americans while he was in the area. Gertrude Three Finger is the young woman in this photo. She was a member of the Cheyenne tribe and is wearing a traditional outfit that is accessorized with elk teeth.

Irwin photographed Gertrude more than once, this photo was one that was printed using an albumen print. You can see it in real life at the University of Oklahoma's library.

Cynthia Ann Parker, also known as **Naduah (Comanche: Narua)** was a white woman who was notable for having been captured at about age nine, by a Comanche war band and adopted into the tribe. Twenty-four years later she was discovered and taken captive by Texas Rangers, at approximately age 33, and unwillingly taken back to European-American society. Her Comanche name means "someone found" in English.

Thoroughly assimilated as Comanche, Parker had married Peta Nocona, a chief. They had three children together, including son Quanah Parker, who became the last free Comanche chief.

Parker became assimilated into the tribe. She was adopted by a Tenowish Comanche couple, who raised her as their own daughter. She became Comanche in every sense. She married Peta Nocona, a chief. They enjoyed a happy marriage. As a tribute to his great affection to her, he never took another wife, although it was traditional for chieftains to have several wives. They had three children: one was Quanah, who became the last free Comanche chief.

Muscogee actor Will (Sonny) Sampson is most known for his role in "One Flew Over the Cuckoo's Nest" playing opposite Jack Nicholson, will be posthumously inducted into the Oklahoma Movie Hall of Fame at the Roxy Theater in Muskogee Oklahoma.

"Will was a dear friend, as was his son Tim and sister. Am happy that he is receiving this honor today. I had the privilege to work with Will in the miniseries 'Mystic Warrior' (1984). He gave me advice while working on this series. I was set to have the lead role and Will was to be cast as the medicine man. What happened was ABC ended up casting the lead role to an Irish actress, dyed her hair black and put contact lenses in and Will's character went to an Italian actor.' Will was a kind man and very supportive of my work. In 1983, he founded the American Indian Registry for the Performing Arts for Native American actors." - Joanelle Romero (RNCI Founder/actress/director/producer).

In addition to his incredible performance as the apparent deaf and mute Chief Bromden in "One Flew Over the Cuckoo's Nest," he also played Crazy Horse in the 1977 western "The White Buffalo," as well as Taylor in "Poltergeist II: The Other Side" and Ten Bears in 1976's "The Outlaw Josey Wales."For 20 years Sonny competed in rodeos, his specialty being bronco busting. He was also an artist, his artwork has been shown at the Gilcrease Museum and the Philbrook Museum of Art.During the filming of "The White Buffalo," Sonny halted production by refusing to act when he discovered that producers had hired white actors to portray Native Americans for the film.

The Piegan are one of the three groups that make up the Blackfoot Confederacy. They were the most dominant group in the northern Great Plains during the 19th century. The Piegan used to live in the Rocky Mountain Front, the place where the Rocky Mountains meet the Plains, for thousands of years before moving further into the Plains. They lived a nomadic and semi-agricultural life before the introduction of guns and horses into their society. The introduction of European goods facilitated the hunting of bison and prompted them to move into the northern Plains, where they went on to dominate the region. Their first encounter with white people occurred in the 1787-88 winter, when they let a fur trader James Gaddy and an explorer David Thompson camp with them. The Piegan numbered around 3,700 in 1858, a small population previously decimated by smallpox and starvation. Today there are around 27,000 full blooded Piegan Blackfeet, and around 80,000 of Piegan descent. The Piegan population is split between the U.S.-Canada border, as they were historically forced to pick a side when the borders were drawn. These divisions, however, only physically split up a nation, as the bonds of its people are that of blood and are thus stronger than any barrier between them.

The Arapaho people lived spread out across Wyoming and Colorado. They have a very strong oral tradition and share their tribal stories with their people and younger generations to keep their transitions alive. Their second love was agriculture.

They became a nomadic tribe in the 1830s, living in teepees and riding their horses while working hard on their fields, growing crops like beans and corn. They would often trade goods with the Arikara and Mandan tribes. Everything they wore had meaning, including the beads on their garbs and the feathers in their headpieces.

Chief John Smith (likely born between 1822 and 1826, though allegedly as early as 1784; died February 6, 1922) was an Ojibwe (Chippewa) Indian who lived in the area of Cass Lake, Minnesota. In 1920, two years before his death, he appeared as the main feature in a motion picture exhibition that toured the US, featuring aged Native Americans.

At the ripe age of 137, White Wolf a.k.a. Chief John Smith is considered the oldest Native American to have ever lived, 1785–1922.

The Minneapolis Morning Tribune obituary says Ga-Be-Nah-Gewn-Wonce (variously known as Kay-bah-nung-we-way, Sloughing Flesh, Wrinkled Meat or plain old — well, really old — John Smith) was reputed to be 137 years old when he died. Whatever his precise age, his well-lined face indicates a man who led a long and full life.

"Pi'tamaka also known as "Brown Weasel Woman" was born into **the Piikáni Piegan Tribe of the Blackfeet Nation.** She was the eldest of two sisters and two brothers. As a girl, she began to show less interest in traditional female roles and more interest in hunting and the games her brothers played. Her father, a well-respected warrior of the tribe, indulged her interest and taught her to hunt and fight.

"She loved learning the ways of a warrior and soon gave up the work of the household in exchange for hunting buffalo with her father. During one of these buffalo hunts, the group of hunters encountered an enemy war party and when they retreated at top speed to escape their enemies, her father had his horse shot out from under him and he was injured. Although it was very dangerous, Brown Weasel Woman turned back, picked up her father and escaped. One of the bravest deeds a warrior could perform was to face the enemy while riding back to rescue someone who was left behind. So when she returned to camp, the people honored her for being courageous.

"Soon after, her mother became very ill and, because she was the oldest child, Brown Weasel Woman took over the chores of the household to help her mother. Although she was an excellent home maker, she did not have any interest in doing any of it. She enjoyed the men's activities of hunting and war much more. Although many of the men took an interest in her, she did not have any interest in having a boyfriend or becoming married. "The turning point of Brown Weasel Woman's life came when her father was killed during a war party and her mother died soon afterwards. Brown Weasel Woman suddenly became responsible for her brothers and sisters. She took on the role as the head of the family which meant that she hunted for and protected her family. Because of this new responsibility, a widowed woman moved in to help with the household chores and to help teach her brothers and sisters.

"Brown Weasel Woman's first war adventure was against the Crows who had stolen some Blackfeet horses. It took the war party several days to get to Crow country, but when they arrived, the Blackfeet were successful at stealing many of the Crow's horses. Brown Weasel Woman stole eleven horses by herself. Although the Crows chased them for a while, the Blackfeet got safely back to their camp.

"On the way back to the camp, Brown Weasel Woman was on watch duty from the top of a butte, while the others rested in a hidden location. She saw two enemies approaching, and before she could reach the men to warn them of the danger, the enemies were ready to round up and steal their horses. Brown Weasel Woman ran down the butte with her rifle and grabbed the rope of the herd's lead horse to keep the rest from running away. The enemies saw that she was a woman and began to close in on her because they did not expect any trouble from her. Brown Weasel Woman shot the enemy who carried a rifle and forced the other one to turn and run. The men were very impressed by her courage of saving the horses and killing an enemy.

"During the summer, when the tribes gathered and the warriors told of their many adventures, the Piikáni Chief told Brown Weasel Woman to share hers. This was a highly unusual thing for a woman to be asked, but after doing so, the chief bestowed upon her the name Pi'tamaka (Running Eagle) as a sign of respect and honor."

Elsie Vance Chestuen was born in 1873, her Indian name was Chestuen. Her mother was Dilth-cley-ih, daughter of the Apache Chief Bidu-ya, Beduiat known as Victorio. Elsie's father is unknown, her mother married

Mangus who was the son of Mangas Coloradas, Chief of the Chiricahua Apaches.Elsie was sent to the Carlisle Indian Industrial School on 4th November 1886 when she was 13 years old,she was enrolled as Elsie Vanci. Carlisle and other schools like this have been a contentious issue with the Native Americans, many say that children were forced to leave their families at very young age. They were forced to change their Indian names and give up their cultures, languages, and religion.

Elsie was only at Carlisle school for 3 years. On the 30th of May 1889, when she was 16 years old, she was sent to Alabama due to illness, she stayed with another Indian lady called Mollie. Elsie must have moved back to her home at some stage, as she died at Fort Sill on April 15th 1898, from tuberculosis. She was 26 years old, Elsie Vance Chestuen, is buried at the Beef Creek Apache Cemetery in Oklahoma Tatanka Means, Oglala. Lakota.....the son of Russell Means.

Tatanka Means was born on February 19, 1985 in Rapid City, South Dakota, USA as Tatanka Wanbli Sapa Xila Sabe Means. He is known for his work on A Million Ways to Die in the West (2014), The Host (2013) and Maze Runner: The Scorch Trials (2015). He's also a great comedian.

Tatanka Means Trivia:

His name means "Male Buffalo" in Lakota, he speaks Lakota.

He was the 2001 USA National Boxing Champion at age of 16.

His skills include horseback riding and powwow dancing.

He is featured in 2006 Indian Male calendar.

He is the son of American Indian activist and actor Russell Means.

His mother's name is Gloria.

Has a half brother named Scott.

His younger brother is Nataani Nez Means First

cousin of Jeremiah Bitsui.

He is a professional stand-up comedian.
He is an enrolled member of the Oglala Lakota Nation in Pine Ridge South Dakota.

> *He was raised in Chinle, AZ on the Navajo Nation Indian Reservation.*
>
> *Won Best Actor in a Leading Role award at the Red Nation Film Festival (2012) for his role as Wolf in Judy Blume's Tiger Eyes.*
>
> *Won Best Actor award at the Dream speakers Film Festival for his role as Jim Sundell in Derby Kings (2013).*
>
> *Won Best Actor award at the Nevada International Film Festival for his role as Jim Sundell in Derby Kings (2013).*

Tatanka has appeared in Into the West as "Crazy Horse," The Burrowers as "Tall Ute," Banshee as "Hoyt Rivers," A Million Ways to Die in the West, Maze Runner: The Scorch Trials, The Host, Saints & Strangers, The Night Shift, Neither Wolf Nor Dog, and Graves.

Chief Big Tree was a Kiowa warrior and chief was born in 1850. Here's what the authorities at the Texas State Historical Association have to say about him:

> **Big Tree (Ado-Eete), Kiowa warrior**, *chief, and cousin of Satanta, was born somewhere in the Kiowa domain at the time when pressures from the expanding non-native population were threatening the tribe's traditional way of life. By the late 1860s the embattled Kiowas were forced to seek an accord with whites. The agreement, arrived at during the Medicine Lodge Treaty Council in 1867, forced Big Tree and the Kiowas to move to a reservation in southwestern Oklahoma. Frustrated by the confinement, Big Tree came under the sway of leaders of the tribal war faction at an early age. He joined Satank, Lone Wolf,qqv and Satanta in raids on settlements inside Indian Territory and across the Red River in Texas. He reputedly was involved in an abortive attack on Fort Sill in June 1870 but really gained notoriety as a result of his participation in the Warren Wagontrain Raid, or Salt Creek Massacre, of May 18, 1871.*
>
> *On August 22, 1874, a number of Kiowas, led by Satanta and Big Tree, combined with Quahadis and skirmished with troops during ration distribution at Anadarko Agency, Indian Territory. From there the Indians moved onto the Llano Estacado in Texas, where, on September 9, 1874, a party of 200 Kiowas, including Lone Wolf, Satanta, and Big Tree, attacked Gen. Nelson A. Miles's supply train, some thirty-six wagons escorted by a company of the Fifth Infantry*

and a detachment of the Sixth Cavalry. For three days the army held off the Indians until, unable to overwhelm the soldiers, the Kiowas drew off and returned home.

Big Tree remained imprisoned at Fort Sill until the Kiowas were finally defeated in December 1874. After his release, he spent the remainder of his life counseling peace and acceptance of the white man's ways. His new direction was especially manifested in his drive to discredit the revivalist doctrine preached by the prophet Poinka in 1887 and in his decision not to participate in the Kiowa Ghost Dance of 1890. He was among those who requested a missionary and was instrumental in establishing the first Baptist mission on the Kiowa reservation. By 1897 Big Tree's conversion was complete; he became a member of the Rainy Mountain Baptist Church and served as a deacon for thirty years. He died at his home in Anadarko on November 13, 1929, his last act of leadership being his unsuccessful opposition to the allotment of Kiowa lands in 1901. He was buried near his home in the Rainy Mountain Cemetery.

Black Eagle, an Oglala Lakota medicine man (1932), was much more than a shaman and healer. These medicine men were also the humorous men who brought culture and joy to their tribe. These men were also named Heyókȟa. They preferred to do everything backwards, including riding horses backwards, or wearing their clothes inside out.

The purpose of these men was to make the people of the tribe question things, knowing that things were done one way, but could be done another. They worked to remove hate and fears from their people.

Sioux Chief Long Wolf and Family (circa 1880) went to London with Buffalo Bill's show and died there in 1892. Thanks to the struggles of a British homemaker, his remains will be returned home. On May 28, 1997 William D. Montalbano of Bromsgrove, England wrote, "After a restless century in a melancholy English graveyard, the remains--and the spirit--of a Sioux chief named Long Wolf are returning to his ancestral home in America because one stranger cared. The stranger is a 56-year-old English homemaker named Elizabeth Knight, who lives in a small row house with her husband, Peter, a roof repairer in this Worcestershire village near Birmingham. "I am a very ordinary sort of person," she said. The sort who writes letters, not e-mail, who makes no long-distance phone calls, has no fancy degrees, has little worldly experience, who never gets her name in the papers. The sort who turns detective and historian and raises a transatlantic fuss because her heart is moved and her sense of fair play is outraged. This is the story of how heirs of Middle England and the Wild West have joined forces to fulfill a dying wish made more than a century ago.

For Knight, the story began the day in 1991 that she bought an old book in a market near her house. There was a 1923 story by a Scottish adventurer named R. B. Cunninghame Graham that began this way: "In a lone corner of a crowded London cemetery, just at the end of a smoke-stained GrecoRoman colonnade under a poplar tree, nestles a neglected grave." In the grave, under a stylized cross and the howling image of his namesake, lies Long Wolf. He died at 59 in a London hospital on June 11, 1892, the victim of bronchial pneumonia contracted in what was then a crowded, dark, gloomy, industrial city as far as anywhere on Earth from the Great Plains of North America. "I was moved. I kept taking the book down, imagining Long Wolf lying there amid the ranks of pale faces:

> **Flying Hawk** says of himself, "I was born four miles below where Rapid City now is, in 1852, about full moon in March. My father was Black Fox and my mother's name was Iron Cedarwoman. My father was a chief. In a fight with the Crows he was shot below the right eye with an arrow; it was so deep that it could not be pulled out, but had to be pushed through to the ear. My tribe was the Ogalalla clan. Our family roamed on hunts for game and enemies all about through the country and to Canada. My father died when he was eighty years old. He had two wives and they were sisters. My mother was the youngest and had five children. The other wife had eight children, making thirteen in all. Kicking Bear was my full brother, and Chief Black Fox was my half-brother and was named for our father. When ten years old I was in my first battle on the Tongue River—Montana now. It was an Overland Train of covered wagons who had soldiers with them. The way it was started, the soldiers fired on the Indians, our tribe, only a few of us. We went to our friends and told them we had been fired on by the soldiers, and they surrounded the train and we had a fight with them. I do not know how many we killed of the soldiers, but they killed four of us.
>
> After that we had a good many battles, but I did not take any scalps for a good while. I cannot tell how many I killed when a young man. "When I was twenty years old we went to the Crows and stole a lot

of horses. The Crows discovered us and followed us all night. When daylight came we saw them behind us. I was the leader. We turned back to fight the Crows. I killed one and took his scalp and a field glass and a Crow necklace from him. We chased the others back a long way and then caught up with our own men again and went on. It was a very cold winter. There were twenty of us and each had four horses. We got them home all right and it was a good trip that time. We had a scalp dance when we got back. "We soon moved camp. One night the Piegans came and killed one of our people. We trailed them in the snow all night. At dawn we came up to them. One Piegan stopped. The others went on. We surrounded the one. He was a brave man. I started for him. He raised his gun to shoot when I was twenty feet away. I dropped to the ground and his bullet went over me; then I jumped on him and cut him through below the ribs and scalped him. We tied the scalp to a long pole. The women blacked their faces and we had a big dance over it. "The next day I started out again with some men and we ran into a Crow camp. We got into that camp by moonlight, but we got caught. They started to fire on us. We all ran into a deep gulch. We got out, but when it was day we saw them coming with a herd 'of horses, going back to the Crow camp. We got in front of them and hid in a hollow. When I looked out I saw they had Sioux horses which they had stolen from our camp. "A big Crow was ahead and the others were riding behind. I took a good aim at the big Crow and shot him in the chest. The rest of them left the horses and ran away. The big Crow was still living. I took another shot at him, then I took his scalp. We took all the horses they had stolen. There were sixty-nine head that time. "Some time after we went to hunt buffalo. All the men went on this hunt. While we were butchering the kill some Piegans were coming. We went to meet them and had a fight. Some missed their 'horses and were running on foot. I was on a good fast horse. I ran over one and knocked him down and fell on him and scalped him alive (ugh). Another one of my people was close by and he shot the one I scalped. This fight was below where Fort Peck is. "More Piegans came. More of them than us. We were attacked by the Piegans. I kneeled down beside a sage bush. A Piegan shot at me but missed. I shot at him and hit his horse. It went down. Then I turned back and ran into a Piegan. Four of them were butchering buffaloes. I shot at them but missed. The Piegans ran and left their horses, and I took them all. We killed three of the Piegans. They shot one of our horses through the head. The fight was over and the Piegans went to a hill. "On the way back we ran into a lot of Crows and we had a fight on horseback. We chased them but no one was killed. Flying Hawk.

Shoshone Warrior Gor-osimp (photographed between 1884-1885). In honor of the indigenous people of North America who have influenced our indigenous medicine and spirituality by virtue of their being a member of a tribe from the Western Region through the Plains including the beginning of time until tomorrow.

Cher was born Cherilyn Sarkisian (May 20, 1946). In 1961, Cher's mother Holt married bank manager Gilbert LaPiere, who adopted Cher (under the name **Cheryl LaPiere)** and her sister Georganne, and enrolled them at Montclair College Preparatory School, a private school in Encino, whose students were mostly from affluent families. The school's upper-class environment presented a challenge for Cher; biographer Connie Berman wrote, "[she] stood out from the others in both her striking appearance and outgoing personality." A former classmate commented, "I'll never forget seeing Cher for the first time. She was so special ... She was like a movie star, right then and there ... She said she was going to be a movie star and we knew she would." Despite not being an excellent student, Cher was intelligent and creative, according to Berman. She earned high grades, excelling in French and English classes. As an adult, she discovered that she had dyslexia. Cher's unconventional behavior stood out: she performed songs for students during the lunch hours and surprised peers when she wore a midriff-baring top. She later recalled, "I was never really in school. I was always thinking about when I was grown up and famous.

Dust Maker, also known as **Pete Mitchell**, was from the Ponca tribe in Northern Nebraska, 1898. As Comanches were seen and highly regarded as outstanding horsemen, they were also observed by other people to have a copper-color about their skin with black eyes and hair. Comanches were well-built and seemingly of medium height. The men possessed just a little bit of facial hair but had a very prominent nose. They wore buckskin moccasins, leggings, and a breech clout. In colder times, a blanket or a bison robe would be worn over the man's shoulders.

With regard to adornments worn by young men, the Comanche elder Frank Chekovi related that pierced ears were sought after when an individual wanted to dress up.

The young man went to the tipi of an experienced person who knew how to pierce. One very red-hot needle was used. A greased straw was placed in the hole once it had been pierced. If more than one hole was desired on an ear, they were all done at the same time in order to properly heal. For instance, some young men liked shell beads and others rings that were worn along the edge of an ear. Copper wire bands could be worn about the wrist and the ear decorations on men were commonplace.

A remarkable picture of the graceful Minnie Too-sh-pip-pen and the very handsome Slim Tiebo, circa 1900. The Comanche Slim Tiebo would have been around twenty years of age. He was born in 1880 and passed away in 1952. The prominent Comanche Tiebo farmed his land and lived his entire life in the area of Cache, Oklahoma. He is buried at the Post Oak Cemetery, Indiahoma, Oklahoma. Photograph courtesy of the Denver Public Library, Denver, Colorado.

Chief Blue Horse, an Oglala, was born in 1820, SHON-KEE-TOH. His principal object in life was to try to make others happy around him. Oglala Lakota Chief Blue Horse (1822-1908), Sunka Wakan To, was the second son of Old Chief Smoke and Burnt Her Woman, and the biological brother of Chief Big Mouth. Chief Red Cloud was the adopted brother of Chief Blue Horse. Red Cloud was adopted by Old Chief Smoke, his maternal uncle, around 1825 at the age of three after Red Cloud's parents died. Blue Horse and Red Cloud were raised as brothers and mentored by Old Chi.

He witnessed the meeting of **Chief Dull Knife**; The Treaty of Fort Laramie was an agreement between the United States and the Lakota nation, signed in 1868 at Fort Laramie in the Wyoming Territory, guaranteeing to the Lakota ownership of the Black Hills, and further land and hunting rights in South Dakota, Wyoming, and Montana. The Powder River Country was to be henceforth closed to all whites. The treaty ended Red Cloud's War. The treaty included articles intended to "insure the civilisation" of the Lakota; financial incentives for them to farm land and become competitive - and stipulations that minors should be provided with an "English education" at a "mission building". To this end the US government included in the treaty that white teachers, blacksmiths and a farmer, a miller, a carpenter, an engineer and a government agent should take up residence within the reservation. Repeated violations of the otherwise exclusive rights to the land by gold prospectors led to the Black Hills War.

Wanada Parker Page (1882-1970) was born in 1882 in Indian Territory. Her Indian name was Woon-ardy Parker. "Woon-ardy" in Comanche means "Stand Up and Be Strong," because she was weak in the limbs and had to walk on crutches for a long time. Mrs. Page had also been given her mother's name, Weckeah.

She attended Chilocco Indian School, then in 1894 was sent to Carlisle Indian School, Pa. where she remained several years with her half-brother Harold (oldest of Quanah's sons) and her half-sister Neda.

At Carlisle, her name was spelled at first "Juanada" until it was objected that she was not Mexican or Spanish. She was baptized under the name of "Annie" in 1895 at St. John's Episcopal Church in Carlisle, but nobody called her that.

Wanada attended the Fort Sill Indian School for about a year, about 1903, living in a girl's frame dormitory.

In 1908 she married Walter Komah, a Comanche. They went to Mescalero, N.M., where he died of tuberculosis in 1912. Wanada returned to Lawton shortly after that. She worked at Fort Sill Indian School as assistant matron while her sister Alice was a student.

In 1915 she became a nurse's aide at the Fort Sill Indian Hospital and it was during her work there that she met her future husband, Harrison Page. He was a white soldier in the Medical Corps assigned to the Station Hospital at Fort Sill. They commuted by street car during their courtship and were married on Dec. 18, 1916.

In her later years, Mrs. Page attended the first Parker Family Reunion at Fort Parker, Tex., in 1953, when the Indian Parkers of Oklahoma and the white Parkers of Texas held their first annual get-together.

Steve Reevis (August 14, 1962 – December 7, 2017) was a Native American actor and member of the Blackfeet Tribe known for his roles in the films Fargo, Last of the Dogmen, and Dances with Wolves.

Reevis was born in Browning, Montana, to father Lloyd "Curley" and mother Lila Reevis. The fourth oldest of six children, he had two brothers and three sisters. Reevis grew up on the Blackfeet Indian Reservation in Northwestern Montana.

He attended and graduated from Flandreau Indian School in Flandreau, South Dakota. Following high school graduation, he attended Haskell Indian Junior College in Lawrence, Kansas, where he received an associate of arts degree.

Reevis' first movie appearance was with his brother, Tim Reevis, as a stunt rider in the 1987 film War Party. Reevis' first acting role was in 1988 in the Universal Studios film Twins, starring Arnold Schwarzenegger and Danny DeVito. Following Twins, he was cast in a nonspeaking role as a Sioux Warrior in the 1990 Kevin Costner film, Dances with Wolves. Reevis was next cast as Chato, an Apache scout, in Geronimo: An American Legend with fellow-Native actor Wes Studi. In 1995, Reevis played Yellow Wolf in Last of the Dogmen alongside Tom Berenger and Barbara Hershey.

He was cast in the critically acclaimed 1996 film, Fargo as well as the madefor-television movie, Crazy Horse. Reevis was honored with awards for his roles in both movies by First Americans in the Arts (FAITA) in 1996. In 2004, Reevis was once again honored by FAITA for his work on the ABC series Line of Fire.

Reevis appeared in Columbia's 2003 film The Missing, in the 2005 remake of The Longest Yard and in TNT's 2005 miniseries Into the West. Reevis also appeared on Fox's drama series Bones.

Čhetáŋ Kiŋyáŋ - Flying Hawk was an Oglala Lakota warrior, historian, educator and philosopher.

Flying Hawk's life chronicles the history of the Oglala Lakota people through the 19th and early 20th centuries, as he fought to deflect the worst effects of white rule; educate his people and preserve sacred Oglala Lakota land and heritage.

Chief Flying Hawk was a participant in Red Cloud's War and in nearly all of the battles with the U.S. Army during the Great Sioux War of 1876. He fought alongside his first cousin Crazy Horse and his brothers Kicking Bear and Black Fox II in the Battle of the Little Big Horn in 1876, and was present at the death of Crazy Horse in 1877 and the Wounded Knee Massacre of 1890.

Flying Hawk was one of the five warrior cousins who sacrificed blood and flesh for Crazy Horse at the Last Sun Dance of 1877.

Chief Flying Hawk was the author of his commentaries and accounts of the Battle of the Little Big Horn, Crazy Horse and the Wounded Knee Massacre, and of Native American warriors and statesmen from who fought to protect their families, defend the invasion of their lands and preserve their culture.

He was probably the longest standing Wild Wester, traveling for over 30 years throughout the United States and Europe from about 1898 to about 1930. Chief Flying Hawk was an educator and believed public education was essential to preserve Lakota culture. He frequently visited public schools for presentations.

Chief Flying Hawk leaves a legacy of Native American philosophy and his winter count covers nearly 150 years of Lakota history.

Dewey Beard or Wasú Máza ("Iron Hail", 1858–1955) was a Lakota who fought in the Battle of Little Bighorn as a teenager. After George Armstrong Custer's defeat, Wasú Máza followed Sitting Bull into exile in Canada and then back to South Dakota where he lived on the Cheyenne River Indian Reservation.

Cheyenne Dog Soldier, 1840., (no picture) The Dog Soldiers were the Cheyenne Elite, they formed their own bands within the Cheyenne Nation, they often gave their own lives to protect their women and children, they were very much feared by the white Soldiers, and their Native American Foes, Pawnee, Ute, to name but a few, however, they were honored Allies of the Lakota Sioux, and the Arapahoe's, Comanche's and Kiowa's, the mention of the words "Cheyenne Dog Soldier", put Fear into the most hardest of white Soldiers, they are still the most famous warrior society on Earth today.

Crazy Horse, was born on the Republican River about 1845. He was killed at Fort Robinson, Nebraska, in 1877, so that he lived barely thirty-three years.

He was an uncommonly handsome man. While not the equal of Gall in magnificence and imposing stature, he was physically perfect, an Apollo in symmetry. Further more he was a true type of Indian refinement and grace. He was modest and courteous as Chief Joseph; the difference is that he was a born warrior, while Joseph was not. However, he was a gentle warrior, a true brave, who stood for the highest ideal of the Sioux [Lakota.] Notwithstanding all that historians have said of him, it is only fair to judge a man by the estimate of his own people rather than that of his enemies.

In the final months before his surrender in 1877, retreated alone to the Powder River country and pleaded for a vision that would show him how to preserve his people and their homeland.

Compounding the Lakota war chief's grief during that long winter was the ill health of his wife, Black Shawl. As he fasted and prayed in the hills near the present-day Montana-Wyoming line, a red-tailed hawk, his spirit helper, descended with an eagle.

Crazy Horse took the eagle's message to holy men and together they created a healing ceremony. Although Crazy Horse was killed within months of his surrender, Black Shawl — thought at the time to have tuberculosis — lived to be an old woman.

The eagle, chief of birds — the one who could fly the highest and carry messages to and from First Maker — was intricately woven into life on the Northern Plains.

Wes Studi has had one long enjoyable acting career. He was raised in Nofire Hollow Oklahoma, speaking Cherokee only until he started school. At 17 he joined the National Guard and later went to Vietnam. After his discharge, Studi became politically active in American Indian affairs. He participated in Wounded Knee at Pine Ridge Reservation in 1973. Wes is known for his roles as a fierce Native American warrior, such as the Pawnee warrior in Dances with Wolves. In the Last of the Mohicans he plays the Huron named Magua, which was his first major part. Soon after he got the lead role in Geronimo: An American Legend. He was in Skinwalkers, The Lone Ranger, and The Horse Whisperer. He played the Indian out in the desert in The Doors movie, and he was also in Avatar. Studi also plays bass and he and his wife are in a band called Firecat of Discord. Wes Studi also serves as honorary chair of the national endowment campaign, of the Indigenous Language Institute that's working to save Native Languages. He and his family live in Santa Fe New Mexico, and Wes has been in several other movies, TV shows and movies, and mini series. He also received an Academy Honorary Award, becoming the first Native American and the second North American Indigenous person to be honored by the Academy, the first was Buffy Sainte-Marie.

Two Leggins, a chief of the River Crow in the last of the buffalo days, was protected by the medicine of an eagle feather painted with six white spots. It gave him the power to direct the wind, he said in his dictated autobiography.

"After the proper ceremony, the wind would blow from the direction pointed by the feather in my hair," he said. "The six spots meant the owner could cause a sudden hailstorm between myself and a pursuing enemy. Later I used the feather many times and it always worked."

Who could doubt the spiritual power of such a magnificent bird?

Once, on a hunting trip in the Bighorn Mountains, Cheyenne warrior Wooden Leg watched as an eagle swooped down on a buffalo calf and carried it far up a cliff to its nest.

"Ordinarily a capturing eagle would drop its prey from high in the air, so that it would be killed by the fall to the ground," Wooden Leg told his biographer Thomas Marquis. "But this did not happen in this case. As long as we stayed there watching, we could see the buffalo calf standing up there on the cliff and wiggling its tail."

In 1875, at the end of his grueling vision quest on Otter Creek in southeastern Montana, the 17-year-old warrior was presented with an eagle wing bone flute by his father.

"It was to be worn about my neck, suspended at the mid-breast by a buckskin thong during times of danger," Wooden Leg said. "If I were threatened with imminent harm I had but to put it to my lips and cause it to send out its soothing notes. That would ward off every evil design upon me.

It was my mystic protector. It was my medicine."

Warriors sought the courage and protection of the eagle in battle and wore eagle feathers as a testimony of honors earned. Each tribal group had its own traditions.

"An eagle's feather worn in the hair was a mark of distinction and told the world that the wearer had counted coups," Crow Chief Plenty Coups said in his biography by Frank Linderman.

If a Crow warrior was wounded counting coups — a lesser honor than returning from the field of battle without a scratch — the feather would be painted red to show that he bled, Plenty Coups said.

Four eagle feathers were attached to the shield given to Sitting Bull by his father after exploits against the Crow at Powder River. The four feathers boasted of his success in all four directions.

Warriors couldn't just claim to have counted coups. The deeds had to be witnessed and attested before the right to wear an eagle feather was earned.

Even after intertribal warfare ceased and tribes have been relegated to reservations, the eagle continues to hold its power.

Chief Joseph Medicine Crow No 106, a Crow historian and World War II veteran, wrote in "Counting Coups" that before he went to war, a Shoshone sun dance chief gave him a white eagle feather. When battle loomed, he stuffed it inside his helmet. He credits the feather with protecting him during the bloody invasion of Germany.

Then he passed the feather on to one of his cousins.

It was carried by members of Medicine Crow's family to Africa, Germany, Italy and later to Korea.

The Omaha Actor **Rodney A. Grant** was abandoned by his parents, and raised by grandparents on the Omaha Rez. He starred in "Dances with Wolves", "Geronimo, an American Legend" "Hawkeye" and a list of other films. Mr Grant illustrates a clash of cultures here at an awards ceremony, by appearing in both the customary evening attire and a traditional headdress. Blessed are those who know themselves, and remember where they came from.

Traditionally, the people now known as **Cherokee** refer to themselves as Aniyunwiya (ah nee yun wee yah), a name usually translated as "the Real People," sometimes "the Original People." The Cherokee never had princesses. This is a concept based on European folktales and has no reality in Cherokee history and culture. In fact, Cherokee women were very powerful. They owned all the houses and fields, and they could marry and divorce as they pleased. Kinship was determined through the mother's line.

Clan mothers administered justice in many matters. Beloved women were very special women chosen for their outstanding qualities. As in other aspects of Cherokee culture, there was a balance of power between men and women. Although they had different roles, they both were valued.

The Cherokee never lived in tepees. Only the nomadic Plains tribes did. The Cherokee were southeastern woodland natives, and in the winter they lived in houses made of woven saplings, plastered with mud and roofed with poplar bark. In the summer they lived in open-air dwellings roofed with bark.

The Cherokee have never worn feathered headdresses except to please tourists. These long headdresses were worn by Plains Natives and were made popular through Wild West shows and Hollywood movies. Cherokee men traditionally wore a feather or two tied at the crown of the head. In the early 18th century, Cherokee men wore cotton trade shirts, loincloths, leggings, front-seam moccasins, finger-woven or beaded belts, multiple pierced earrings around the rim of the ear, and a blanket over one shoulder. At that time, Cherokee women wore mantles of leather or feathers, skirts of leather or woven mulberry bark, front-seam moccasins, and earrings pierced through the earlobe only. By the end of the 18th century, Cherokee men were dressing much like their white neighbors. Men were wearing shirts, pants, and trade coats, with a distinctly Cherokee turban. Women were wearing calico skirts, blouses, and shawls. Today Cherokee people dress like other Americans, except for special occasions, when the men wear ribbon shirts with jeans and moccasins, and the women wear tear dresses with corn beads, woven belts, and moccasins.

•The Eastern Band of Cherokee Indians (EBCI) are descended from Cherokee people who had taken land under the Treaty of 1819 and were allowed to remain in North Carolina; from those who hid in the woods and mountains until the U.S. Army left; and from those who turned around and walked back from Oklahoma. By 1850 they numbered almost a thousand. Today the Eastern Band includes about 11,000 members, while the Cherokee Nation in Oklahoma claims more than 100,000 members, making the Cherokee the largest tribe in the United States.

•Cherokee arts and crafts are still practiced: basket-weaving, pottery, carving, finger-weaving, and beadwork.

•The Cherokee language is spoken as a first language by fewer than a thousand people and has declined rapidly because of the policies of federally operated schools. However, since the tribe has begun operation of their own schools, Cherokee language is being systematically taught in the schools.

•Traditional Cherokee medicine, religion, and dance are practiced privately. •There have never been Cherokee shamans. Shamanism is a foreign concept to North America. The Cherokee have medicine men and women."aho" is not a Cherokee word and Cherokee speakers never use it. Most are actually offended by the misuse of this word. It's not some kind of universal Native word used by all tribes, as many believe. Each individual tribe have their own languages. We can respect these languages by using them correctly or not at all.

- In order to belong to one of the seven Cherokee clans, your mother had to have been/be Cherokee and her clan is passed on to you. If the maternal line has been broken by a non Cherokee or someone had all sons, you have no clan, which is the case with many today.

- There is only one Cherokee tribe that consist of three bands. The Cherokee Nation of Oklahoma, United Keetoowah Band of Oklahoma and the Eastern Band of Cherokee Indians of North Carolina. All others who claim a different band than one of the three above are not considered Cherokee and are a direct threat to Cherokee tribal sovereignty. In fact, to be Cherokee, one must be registered with the tribe, as Cherokee is a citizenship granted through documentation. One can have Native DNA but is not considered Cherokee until they are a registered tribal citizen. Via N. Bear Cherokee man North Carolina.

The **Nez-Percés,** Nimíipuu, are an Amerindian tribe of the Penutian group who lived in the Columbia Plateau of the Pacific Northwest region at the time of the Lewis and Clark expedition. The memory of the Nez-Percés remains intact through the breeding and selection of the appaloosa horse, native to the Palouse River, and their heroic resistance during their escape over several thousand kilometers under the leadership of Chief Joseph.

Sarah Rector was born in 1902 in Creek Nation in the community of Twine, Oklahoma. She came from very humble beginnings, but later became the wealthiest Black girl in the country at the young age of 11. Her family were African American members of the Muscogee Creek Nation in Indian Territory.

Her grandparents had been enslaved by Creek Tribe members, but after the Civil War, they were entitled to land allotments under the Dawes Allotment Act of 1887. When Indian territory integrated with Oklahoma territory to form the state of Oklahoma in 1907, hundreds of Black children referred to back then as "Creek Freedmen minors," were each granted 160 acres of land.

Rector's allotment was located in the middle of the Glenn Pool oil field and was initially valued at about $550. In 1911, her father decided to lease his daughter's piece of land to a major oil company to help pay for the property taxes. And then in 1913, everything changed.

According to Searching for Sarah Rector: The Richest Black Girl in America by Tonya Bolden, an independent driller struck oil that started bringing in 2,500 barrels or 105,000 gallons per day. Rector, still being the owner of the land, began earning more than $300 a day (the equivalent of about $7,500 a day in our time).

Suddenly, she began getting a lot of national attention from newspapers all over the country. For example, The Kansas City Star published the headline, "Millions to a Negro Girl – Sarah Rector, 10-Year Old, Has Income of $300 A Day From Oil." Meanwhile, another newspaper, The Savannah Tribune, published the headline, "Oil Well Produces Neat Income – Negro Girl's $112,000 A Year."

Rector quickly became famous and naturally started receiving all kinds of request for loans, donations, and even marriage proposals.

Sadly though, there was a law at the time that required wealthy Native Americans and African Americans who were citizens of Indian Territory to be assigned a "well-respected" white guardian. As a result, Rector's guardianship was turned over to a white man named T.J. Porter.

But reportedly W.E.B. Du Bois and the NAACP got involved to protect her wealth and well-being, and were able to successfully do so. She later went on to own one of the first Black-owned auto dealerships in the country, and reportedly enjoyed her wealth until the day she died!

The **Kiowa people** were a nomadic group who became a tribe at approximately 1650. They were located in the northern basin of the Missouri River. They eventually moved to the Black Hills, where they shared the land with the Crow tribe.

The tribe moved about down to the area of the Red River in Arkansas so that they could stay away from tribes who were trying to take over their land and eventually made an alliance with the Comanche tribe in 1807.

Sioux are a broad alliance of North American Indian peoples who spoke three related languages within the Siouan language family. The name Sioux is an abbreviation of Nadouessioux ("Adders"; i.e., enemies), a name originally applied to them by the Ojibwa. The Santee, also known as the Eastern Sioux, were Dakota speakers and comprised the Mdewkanton, Wahpeton, Wahpekute, and Sisseton. The Yankton, who spoke Nakota, included the Yankton and Yanktonai. The Teton, also referred to as the Western Sioux, spoke Lakota and had seven divisions—the Sihasapa, or Blackfoot; Brulé (Upper and Lower); Hunkpapa; Miniconjou; Oglala; Sans Arcs; and Oohenonpa, or Two-Kettle.

Before the middle of the 17th century, the Santee Sioux lived in the area around Lake Superior, where they gathered wild rice and other foods, hunted deer and buffalo, and speared fish from canoes. Prolonged and continual warfare with the Ojibwa to their east drove the Santee into what is now southern and western Minnesota, at that time the territory of the agricultural Teton and Yankton. In turn, the Santee forced these two groups from Minnesota into what are now North and South Dakota. Horses were becoming common on the Plains during this period, and the Teton and Yankton abandoned agriculture in favor of an economy centered on the nomadic hunting of bison.

Traditionally the Teton and Yankton shared many cultural characteristics with other nomadic Plains Indian societies. They lived in tepees, wore clothing made from leather, suede, or fur, and traded buffalo products for corn (maize) produced by the farming tribes of the Plains. The Sioux also raided those tribes frequently, particularly the Mandan, Arikara, Hidatsa, and Pawnee, actions that eventually drove the agriculturists to ally themselves with the U.S. military against the Sioux tribes. Sioux men acquired status by performing brave deeds in warfare; horses and scalps obtained in a raid were evidence of valour. Sioux women were skilled at porcupine-quill and bead embroidery, favoring geometric designs; they also produced prodigious numbers of processed bison hides during the 19th century, when the trade value of these "buffalo robes" increased dramatically. Community policing was performed by men's military societies, the most significant duty of which was to oversee the buffalo hunt. Women's societies generally focused on fertility, healing, and the overall well-being of the group. Other societies focused on ritual dance and shamanism. Religion was an integral part of all aspects of Sioux life, as it was for all Native American peoples. The Sioux recognized four powers as presiding over the universe, and each power in turn was divided into hierarchies of four. The buffalo had a prominent place in all Sioux rituals. Among the Teton and Santee the bear was also a symbolically important animal; bear power obtained in a vision was regarded as curative, and some groups enacted a ceremonial bear hunt to protect warriors before their departure on a raid. Warfare and supernaturalism were closely connected, to the extent that designs suggested in mystical visions were painted on war shields to protect the bearers from their enemies. The annual Sun Dance was the most important religious event. Having suffered from the encroachment of the Ojibwa, the Sioux were extremely resistant to incursions upon their new territory. Teton and Yankton territory included the vast area between the Missouri River and the Teton Mountains and between the Platte River on the south and the Yellowstone River on the north—i.e., all or parts of the present-day states of Montana, North Dakota, South Dakota, Nebraska, Colorado, and Wyoming. This territory was increasingly broached as the colonial frontier moved westward past the Mississippi River in the mid-19th century. The California Gold Rush of 1849 opened a floodgate of travelers, and many Sioux became incensed by the U.S. government's attempt to establish the Bozeman Trail and other routes through the tribes' sovereign lands.

Chief Two Moons (1847–1917), or Ishaynishus (Cheyenne: Éše'he Ôhnéšesêstse), was one of the Cheyenne chiefs who took part in the Battle of the Little Bighorn and other battles against the United States Army. he was the son of Carries the Otter, an Arikara captive who married into the Cheyenne tribe. Perhaps known best for his participation in battles such as the Battle of the Rosebud against General Crook on June 17, 1876, in the Montana Territory, the Battle of Little Big Horn on June 25, 1876 and what would prove to be his last battle, the Battle of Wolf Mountain on January 8, 1877. Two Moons' defeat at Wolf Mountain by General Nelson A. Miles led inevitably to the surrender of his Cheyenne band to Miles at Fort Keogh in April 1877.

After the surrender of his Cheyenne band, Two Moons enlisted as an Indian Scout under General Miles. As a result of Two Moons' pleasant personality, the friendliness that he showed towards the whites, as well as his ability to get along with the military, General Miles appointed him head Chief of the Cheyenne Northern Reservation. As head Chief, Two Moons played a crucial role in the surrender of Chief Little Cow's Cheyenne band at Fort Keogh.

Two Moons traveled on multiple occasions to Washington, D.C., to discuss and fight for the future of the Northern Cheyenne people and to better the conditions that existed on the reservation. In 1914, Two Moons met with President Woodrow Wilson to discuss these matters. Two Moons was one of the models selected for James Fraser's famous Buffalo Nickel.

Brenda Schad, model and actress Brenda Schad is Choctaw and Cherokee. Brenda has appeared on the cover of Cosmopolitan UK, Vogue, ELLE and GQ UK magazines. She's also made a few movies, Awake (2007), Head Over Heels (2001) and D.R.E.A.M. Team (1999 TV movie).

When **Chief Running Antelope** was born near the Grand River, presently South Dakota, in 1821, few white men were in the area. Consequently, he grew up in the old traditions of his people. He learned to ride and hunt, and later went on horse-stealing expeditions and war parties and joined the secret societies. By the time he reached manhood things had changed. The whites were more numerous, and the Indians were forced to adapt to the new conditions. Many Sioux took up arms and became strong in warfare; the Hunkpapas, one of the smaller bands of the Tetons, became one of the strongest. Running Antelope, however, was one of the first Hunkpapas to reject the warpath and become a friend of the whites. Running Antelope, in his earlier years, was closely allied with Sitting Bull, who was eleven years his junior. Running Antelope, a band chief, was prominent among the Lakota. In 1851, Running Antelope was elected one of four "shirt wearers" of the Hunkpapa. A shirt wearer served to intercede between the council and the headmen and akicita who carried out tribal policy and decisions. He was a brave warrior and accomplished diplomat. A great council with the Sioux was called at Fort Laramie and Fort Rice in 1868. Running Antelope signed the Treaty of 1868 at Fort Rice. It was often said that Running Antelope was the greatest orator of the Sioux Nation. He attended the Fort Laramie, Fort Rice and Fort Peck treaty councils. Under the influence of James McLaughlin, he became a dominant leader of the reservation Hunkpapa people at the Grand River Agency. He was enrolled in 1868 at Grand River Agency, later part of Standing Rock reservation in North and South Dakota. After the allotment period, Running Antelope established a settlement of about sixty families in the Grand River valley and opened a store. In his later years, he regretted signing the 1868 Treaty and longed for the time when the Lakota were free, and realigned with Sitting Bull. Late in 1880, the followers of Sitting Bull began to return from exile in Canada and in the spring of 1881, Running Antelope was enlisted as a scout in the army to go to Fort Buford to escort Gall and his followers to Standing Rock. He was chosen to lead the last great Sioux buffalo hunt in June, 1882. A large herd was sighted about a hundred miles west of Fort Yates, and a hunting party of 2,000 men, women and children left the fort on June 10. The next morning the herd numbering approximately 50,000 buffalo was sighted and the hunt was on. About 2,000 were killed the first day, and the camp moved up to the scene of the hunt and the butchering began. The next day another 3,000 were killed and the camp settled in near a creek to jerk the meat and prepare pemmican. As usual when meat was plentiful, the labors of the Indian camp were lightened by feasting. In 1899, Running Antelope was pictured on the Five-Dollar Silver Certificate. He died between June 30, 1896 and June 30, 1897. He is buried at the Long

Hill Cemetery east of Little Eagle, South Dakota. On the 1885 Standing Rock ration list He had 10 lodges and 42 people in his care.

Mary Frances Thompson Fisher (December 3, 1895 – October 25, 1995), best known as Te Ata, was an actress and citizen of the Chickasaw Nation known for telling Native American stories. She performed as a representative of Native Americans at state dinners before President Franklin D. Roosevelt in the 1930s. She was inducted into the Oklahoma Hall of Fame in 1957 and was named Oklahoma's first State Treasure in 1987.

Te Ata began her early education in a one-room tribal school, but after two years she was sent to Bloomfield Academy, a Chickasaw boarding school for girls. At Bloomfield, she met Muriel Wright, a teacher who became her role model. Te Ata graduated high school from Tishomingo, Oklahoma, where she was salutatorian.

In the fall of 1915, Te Ata began college at the Oklahoma College for Women (now the University of Science and Arts of Oklahoma) in Chickasha, and graduated in 1919. During her time at Oklahoma College for Women, she worked as an assistant in the theater department for theater instructor Frances Dinsmore Davis. It was during this time that Te Ata was first introduced to the stage.

Te Ata's life and likeness have been featured in many books, plays and magazines. In the summer of 1924, Te Ata was featured in McCall's magazine in its "Types of American Beauty" series.

Her life and performances have been commemorated through several different awards. She was the namesake for Lake Te Ata in New York. She was named the Ladies' Home Journal Woman of the Year in 1976. She was inducted into the Oklahoma Hall of Fame in 1957 and named Oklahoma's Official State Treasure in 1987. In 1990, she was inducted into the Chickasaw Hall of Fame.

The Quechan or Yuma (Quechan: Kwatsáan 'those who descended') are an aboriginal American tribe who live on the Fort Yuma Indian Reservation on the lower Colorado River in Arizona and California just north of the Mexican border. Despite their name, they are not related to the Quechua people of the Andes. Members are enrolled into the Quechan Tribe of the Fort Yuma Indian Reservation. The federally recognized Quechan tribe's main office is located in Winterhaven, California. Its operations and the majority of its reservation land are located in California, United States.

The historic Yuman-speaking people in this region were skilled warriors and active traders, maintaining exchange networks with the Pima in southern Arizona, New Mexico, and with peoples of the Pacific coast.

The first significant contact of the Quechan with Europeans was with the Spanish explorer Juan Bautista de Anza and his party in the winter of 1774. Relations were friendly. On Anza's return from his second trip to Alta California in 1776, the chief of the tribe and three of his men journeyed to Mexico City to petition the Viceroy of New Spain for the establishment of a mission. The chief Palma and his three companions were baptized in Mexico City on February 13, 1777. Palma was given the Spanish baptismal name Salvador Carlos Antonio.

Spanish settlement among the Quechan did not go smoothly; the tribe rebelled from July 17–19, 1781 and killed four priests and thirty soldiers. They also attacked and damaged the Spanish mission settlements of San Pedro y San Pablo de Bicuñer and Puerto de Purísima Concepción, killing many. The following year, the Spanish retaliated with military action against the tribe.

After the United States annexed the territories after winning the Mexican–American War, it engaged in the Yuma War from 1850 to 1853 in response to a conflict between the Quechan and Jaeger's Ferry and the Glanton Gang, after the Quechan had established a rival ferry service on the Colorado River. During which, the historic Fort Yuma was built across the Colorado River from the present day Yuma, Arizona.

Pic: Quechan men in western Arizona - circa 1875

Chief Red Fish was a chief of the Oglala Lakota tribe in the 1840s. He had met with the Jesuit missionary Father Peter John De Smet at Fort Pierre in South Dakota in 1848. He asked for De Smet's help in gaining the return of his daughter who had been kidnapped by the Crow after he had made a disastrous unprovoked raid upon them.

Red Fish was a participant in the Fort Laramie Treaty of 1851, where he represented the Miniconjou with his son Lone Horn (c. 1814-1875). He negotiated with Chief Big Robber of the Crow to establish regional boundaries.

Paiute writer and educator Sarah Winnemucca (c. 1880), the daughter and granddaughter of Northern Paiute chiefs, learned English and Spanish as a child, in addition to three Indian dialects. In the 1870s, these abilities led to her serving as an interpreter at Fort McDermitt and then on the Malheur Reservation.

After the Bannock War of 1878 — during which Winnemuccca showed her mettle by working as an army scout, and also rescued a group of Paiute that included her father — some Paiute were forcibly relocated to the Yakima Reservation. Winnemucca, who had already seen how American Indians were at the mercy of sometimes corrupt reservation agents, decided to advocate for Native American land rights and other systemic improvements.

In 1879, Winnemuccca lectured in San Francisco. The next year she met with President Rutherford B. Hayes in Washington, D.C. Winnemucca also became the first Native American woman to produce a published book, Life Among the Piutes: Their Wrongs and Claims (1883). The work included powerful statements such as: "For shame! For shame! You dare to cry out Liberty, when you hold us in places against our will, driving us from place to place as if we were beasts." The U.S. government committed to reforms, including a return to Malheur for the Paiute. However, in the end, nothing changed.

Winnemucca died in 1891. Despite the setbacks she'd encountered, she was a forceful advocate for her people.

According to the origin story of the Apache Indian, in the beginning the world was covered with darkness. There was no sun, no day. The perpetual night had no moon or stars.

There were, however, all manner of beasts and birds. Among the beasts were many hideous, nameless monsters, as well as dragons, lions, tigers, wolves, foxes, beavers, rabbits, squirrels, rats, mice, and all manner of creeping things such as lizards and serpents. Mankind could not prosper under such conditions, for the beasts and serpents destroyed all human offspring. All creatures had the power of speech and were gifted with reason.

There were two tribes of creatures: the birds or the feathered tribe and the beasts. The former were organized wider their chief, the eagle.

These tribes often held councils, and the birds wanted light admitted. This the beasts repeatedly refused to do. Finally, the birds made war against the beasts.

The beasts were armed with clubs, but the eagle had taught his tribe to use bows and arrows. The serpents were so wise that they could not all be killed. One took refuge in a perpendicular cliff of a mountain in Arizona, and his eyes (changed into a brilliant stone) may be seen in that rock to this day. The bears, when killed, would each be changed into several other bears, so that the more bears the feathered tribe killed, the more there were. The dragon could not be killed, either, for he was covered with four coats of horny scales, and the arrows would not penetrate these. One of the most hideous, vile monsters (nameless) was proof against arrows, so the eagle flew high up in the air with a round, white stone, and let it fall on this monster's head, killing him instantly. This was such a good service that the stone was called sacred. They fought for many days, but at last the birds won the victory.

After this war was over, although some evil beasts remained, the birds were able to control the councils, and light was admitted, then mankind could live and prosper. The eagle was chief in this good fight: therefore, his feathers were worn by man as emblems of wisdom, justice, and power.

Among the few human beings that were yet alive was a woman who had been blessed with many children, but these had always been destroyed by the beasts. If by any means she succeeded in eluding the others, the dragon, who was very wise and very evil, would come himself and eat her babes.

After many years a son of the rainstorm was born to her and she dug for him a deep cave. The entrance to this cave she closed and over the spot built a camp fire. This concealed the babe's hiding place and kept him warm. Every day she would remove the fire and descend into the cave, where the child's bed was, to nurse him; then she would return and rebuild the camp fire.

Frequently the dragon would come and question her, but she would say, I have no more children; you have eaten all of them. When the child was larger he would not always stay in the cave, for he sometimes wanted to run and play. Once the dragon saw his tracks. Now this perplexed and enraged the old dragon, for he could not find the hiding place of the boy; but he said that he would destroy the mother if she did not reveal the child's hiding place. The poor mother was very much troubled; she could not give up her child, but she knew the power and cunning of the dragon, therefore she lived in constant fear.

Soon after this the boy said that he wished to go hunting. The mother would not give her consent. She told him of the dragon, the wolves, and serpents; but he said, To-morrow I go.

At the boy's request his uncle (who was the only man then living) made a little bow and some arrows for him, and the two went hunting the next day. They trailed the deer far up the mountain and finally the boy killed a buck. His uncle showed him how to dress the deer and broil the meat. They broiled two hind quarters, one the child and one for his uncle. When the meat was done they placed it on some bushes to cool. Just then the huge form of the dragon appeared. The child was not afraid, but his uncle was so dumb with fright that he did not speak or move.

The dragon took the boy's parcel of meat and went aside with it. He placed the meat on another bush and seated himself beside it. Then he said, This is the child I have been seeking. Boy, you are nice and fat, so when I have eaten this venison I shall eat you. The boy said, No, you shall not eat me, and you shall not eat that meat. So he walked over to where the dragon sat and to where the meat back to his own seat. The dragon said, I like your courage, but you are foolish; what do you think you could do? Well, said the boy, I can do enough to protect myself, as you may bind out. Then the dragon took the meat again, and then the boy retook it. Four times in all the dragon took the meat, and after the fourth time the boy replaced the meat he said, Dragon, will you fight me? The dragon said, Yes, in whatever way you like. The boy said, I will stand one hundred paces distant from you and you may have four shots at me with your bow and arrows, provided that you will then exchange places with me and give me four shots. Good, said the dragon. Stand up.

Bear's Belly, a tribe member of the Arikara people. He was born in 1847 in what we know today to be North Dakota. He was one of the most highly respected fighters in his tribe, where he earned his bear skin that gave him his name in a battle where he killed three bears.

Edward Curtis took a photo of him in 1909, as part of a project that was funded by J.P. Morgan in the amount of $75,000. Curtis wanted to photograph the people but also to document how they led their lives.

Quanah Parker was the last Chief of the Comanche and he never lost a battle to the white man. His tribe roamed over the area where Pampas stands. He was never captured by the Army, but decided to surrender and lead his tribe into the white man's culture, only when he saw that there was no alternative. His was the last tribe in the Staked Plains to come into the reservation system.

Quanah, meaning "fragrant," was born about 1850, son of Comanche Chief Peta Nocona and **Cynthia Ann Parker**, a white girl taken captive during the 1836 raid on Parker's Fort, Texas. Cynthia Ann Parker was recaptured, along with her daughter, during an 1860 raid on the Pease River in northwest Texas. She had spent 24 years among the Comanche, however, and thus never readjusted to living with the whites again.

She died in Anderson County, Texas, in 1864 shortly after the death of her daughter, Prairie Flower. Ironically, Cynthia Ann's son would adjust remarkably well to living among the white men. But first he would lead a bloody war against them.

Oklahoma is home to 39 American Native tribes, many of which were forcibly removed to this area.

White Buffalo (Cheyenne was born in 1862 & died in June 1929) was described in newspaper articles in 1902 as being of striking appearance, as his hair had turned completely white when he was very young. His photo from his Carlisle days, dressed in a suit with a short haircut in the white man's style, shows that to be true. In 1888, when he was 26, he married a full-blood Northern Cheyenne widow. Medicine Woman, who was 30 at the time. She had also been born in Montana as had her parents. On the 1905 Indian Census for their reservation, they had four children listed: Emma White Buffalo, son Receiving Roots, Paul White Buffalo and Pratt White Buffalo - named for the Carlisle School founder. On the 1910 U. S. Federal Census, they are listed with only three of seven surviving children: John White Buffalo, James White Buffalo and Fred White Buffalo. According to the 1910 census, the mother of Medicine Woman also lived with them as well, 76 at the time, widowed and named Siege Woman. Medicine Woman is listed on this census as illiterate, as is her mother. His son, John White Buffalo enlisted for service in World War I. As full blood Cheyenne, both White Buffalo and Medicine Woman received land allotments on the reservation in 1891 in Lincoln Township in present-day Blaine County, Oklahoma. These are listed on several of the Indian Census lists as allotments number 966 and 967. White Buffalo lived to be 67 years old, and passed away on June 23, 1929, per the 1930 Indian census for the reservation. According to his obituary in the Watonga Republican newspaper dated June 27, 1929, he is buried at the Indian Mission Church on the reservation and was survived by his wife and sons.

Chief Crowfoot (of the Blackfoot Confederacy) stood and watched as the white man spread many one dollar bills on the ground, saying, "This is what the white man trades with; this is his buffalo robe. Just as you trade skins, we trade with these pieces of paper."

When the white chief had laid all his money on the ground and shown how much he would give if the Indians would sign a treaty, Crowfoot took a handful of clay, made a ball out of it and put it on the fire.

It did not crack.

Then he said to the white man, Now put your money on the fire and see if it will last as long as the clay.

The white man said, No….my money will burn because it is made of paper.

With an amused gleam in his eyes the old chief said, Oh, your money is not as good as our land, is it?

The wind will blow it away; the fire will burn it; water will rot it. But nothing will destroy our land.

You don't make a very good trade.

Then with a smile, Crowfoot picked up a handful of sand from the river bank, handed it to the white man and said, You count the grains of sand in that while I count the money you give for the land.

The white man said, I would not live long enough to count this, but you can count the money in a few minutes.

Very well, said the wise Crowfoot, our land is more valuable than your money. It will last forever. It will not perish as long as the sun shines and the water flows, and through all the years it will give life to men and animals, and therefore we cannot sell the land. It was put there by the Great Spirit and we cannot sell it because it does not really belong to us.

You can count your money and burn it with a nod of a buffalo's head, but only the Great Spirit can count the grains of sand and the blades of grass on these plains.

As a present we will give you anything you can take with you, but we cannot give you the land."

Jay Silverheels (born Harold Jay Smith; May 26, 1912 – March 5, 1980) was an Indigenous Canadian actor and athlete. He was well known for his role as Tonto, the Native American companion of the Lone Ranger in the American Western television series The Lone Ranger.

Nampeyo (1859-1942) was a Native American potter of Hopi-Tewa origins. She was born on the First Mesa in Arizona to a Hopi father and a Tewa mother that taught her pottery-making. She quickly picked up the craft and became proficient at it, studying the designs of her ancestors from fragments of old pottery. Nampeyo became renowned for her unique designs and found it to be an excellent source of income starting from 1875, the year Thomas Keam, an English trader, opened a trading post on the Hopi reservation. According to Native Partnership: 'Nampeyo used traditional methods to make the pots. She painted them using her own handmade yucca brushes and firing the pots in an outdoor oven. Her style is characterized by geometric figures and pictures of animals and faces. She used a yellowish clay to produce smooth, dense pots. Nampeyo's new designs used the old as a stepping stone, but not as a copy. She is credited with the birth of contemporary Hopi pottery, now called Hano polychrome. Her pottery making became known to traders and anthropologists who came to the Southwest in the 1880s and 1890s.' Nampeyo quickly became famous in artisan circles across the U.S. In 1910 she traveled with her husband Lesso to Chicago for an art exposition. Sadly her years were catching up with her, and by 1920 she was almost completely blind, so her daughters and husband helped her finish her products. She died in 1942, leaving behind her generations of capable potters, and the art of ancient Hopi pottery that she revived.

Chief Dan George was actually a chief of the Tsleil-Waututh Nation in British Columbia, Canada from 1951 to 1963. Also an author and poet, George achieved his first acting job at the age of 60, appearing in the Canadian TV show, Caribou Country. But George's acting career didn't peak until 1970 when he starred in Little Big Man, a role for which he received an Oscar nomination for Best Supporting Actor. Another great role for George was the part of Lone Watie in The Outlaw Josie Wales

(1976), often considered one of the best American Westerns. And George's performance in this American classic could be considered Oscar-worthy as well. George also appeared on TV shows such as Kung Fu. During George's writing career, he was credited with fostering understanding between nonnative and Native Americans, particularly with the release of his book, My Heart Soars.

Walker Calhoun was the youngest of 12 children born to Sally Ann Calhoun and Morgan Calhoun. His father died when he was young.

At the age of 12, Calhoun attended a boarding school in Cherokee, North Carolina, where he was taught the English language. Before that time, he had rarely heard English since his mother did not speak it. During World War II, he was drafted and served as a combat engineer in Germany.

Calhoun started learning Cherokee songs from an early age. He had learned most of the social and sacred songs from his uncle, Will West Long, by the time he was nine years old.

Calhoun founded the Raven Rock Dancers in the 1980s, to help keep traditional Cherokee dances alive within his Big Cove, North Carolina community.

Walker Calhoun was a Cherokee musician, dancer, and teacher. He was known as a medicine man and spiritual leader who worked to preserve the history, religion, and herbal healing methods of his people.

Died: March 28, 2012

The Ute Pass Trail originated just below the springs of Manitou, Colorado, through Ute Pass and into the White River country of Utah. With the Indians dragging their travois along this trail, the route became easier to follow and eventually became a safe route to the Colorado gold fields. Starting in 1860, the mineral rushes to Colorado resulted in large settler migrations that began the first major threat to the Ute way of life. These Ute men pose on horseback as part of the marking ceremony for the Ute Pass Trail on August 29,1912. – Courtesy Southern Ute Cultural Center & Museum.

The Dakota Nation have long been about remaining together and keeping to their roots. Generations have worked to care for one another, from keeping their farms alive, to their households up and running.

Anthropologist Ella Deloria who wrote about the Dakota people shared in 1944, "The Ultimate aim of a Dakota life, stripped of accessories, was quite simple: One must obey kinship rules; one must be a good relative. No Dakota who has participated in that life will dispute that."

Crazy Horse (A Sacred Hero) was born on the Republican River about 1845. He was killed at Fort Robinson, Nebraska, in 1877, so that he lived barely thirty-three years.

He was an uncommonly handsome man. While not the equal of Gall in magnificence and imposing stature, he was physically perfect, an Apollo in symmetry. Furthermore, he was a true type of Indian refinement and grace. He was modest and courteous as Chief Joseph; the difference is that he was a born warrior, while Joseph was not. However, he was a gentle warrior, a true brave, who stood for the highest ideal of the Sioux [Lakota.] Notwithstanding all that biased historians have said of him, it is only fair to judge a man by the estimate of his own people rather than that of his enemies.

The **Ute tribe** is one of the oldest inhabitants in the Southwestern United States, spread out in Colorado and Utah, where they grew their crops and hunted. The Ute people began trading with the Spanish in the 17th century, as well as started to make use of horses to help the tribe spread out further.

When the Mormon communities began arriving in Utah, their lives began to be more complicated. The Ute was then forced out of Utah, an area that got its name from this very tribe. In 1874, the Ute tribe signed the Brunot Treaty, a paper that took away even more of their rights to lands without them knowing.

Warriors are not what you think of as warriors. The warrior is not someone who fights, because no one has the right to take another life. The warrior, for us, is one who sacrifices himself for the good of others. His task is to take care of the elderly, the defenseless, those who cannot provide for themselves, and above all, the children, the future of humanity. —Sitting Bull (c. 1831 - 1890), Hunkpapa Sioux.

"One day, when I was a little girl, my brother and I were on the playground. We saw a beautiful little blond haired girl and we went to play with her. She told my brother 'go home and wash your skin, you're dirty'. My little brother and I ran home crying to our Unci (grandmother). She laid a blanket down and said "Iyotakapi Takoja' (sit down grandchildren) she sat down with us and took a pinch of dirt from the ground and rubbed it into my arm. As it blended into my arm she said 'This is where you come from Takoja, -Unci Maka (Grandmother Earth) This is who we are. You are Lakota and as a Lakota person you are the foundation that holds everything." -Unci Marie Randal.

"In the Lakota tradition, a person who is grieving is considered most waken, most holy.

There's a sense that when someone is struck by the sudden lightning of loss, he or she stands on the threshold of the spirit world. The prayers of those who grieve are considered especially strong, and it is proper to ask them for their help.

You might recall what it's like to be with someone who has grieved deeply. The person has no layer of protection, nothing left to defend. The mystery is looking out through that person's eyes. For the time being, he or she has accepted the reality of loss and has stopped clinging to the past or grasping at the future. In the groundless openness of sorrow, there is a wholeness of presence and a deep natural wisdom."

Iyopeya - to scold, to correct, usually done by hcala.

Wahokunkiya - to give advice, to counsel, again by the hcala.

"Our young do Not understand these concepts, a few do. So when they are being counseled or advised, they think it's being corrected, and they have a tantrum. So some elders just don't do that anymore."-Lakota elder

Ramona Daklugie was born in 1874 in the Chihuahua Territory within the Arizona Territiory. Her parents were Kla esh Chihuahua (Chief Chihuahua Apache) and Ilth gozey (Leah). Because of her parentage, Ramona was a Chiricahua Apache Princess.

After the uprisings in 1885, she was taken prisoner with her tribe by the United States government. They were moved from Florida to Arkansas to Fort Sill, Oklahoma, where they were kept as prisoners of war.

She was sent to the Carlisle Indian School in Carlisle, Pennsylvania where she met her future husband. Ramona married Asa Daklugie in 1898. They had nine children: Maude (1901-1976), Sarah (1902-1910), Lydia (19041955), Blanche (1906-1908), Ramona "Mona" (1909-1920), Maria Georgie (1910-1927), Asa (1912-1918), Patsy (1914-1915), and Marian (19161920).

In 1913, the Daklugie family moved to the Mescalero Indian Reservation in New Mexico where Ramona and Asa spent the rest of their lives.

In 1913, approximately 200 members of the Chiricahua band of Apaches came to the reservation. They had been held prisoner at Fort Sill, Oklahoma since the capture of the famed Apache Geronimo in 1886. All became members of the Mescalero Apache Tribe when it was reorganized under the provisions of the 1934 Indian Reorganization Act.

Ramona passed away on September 25, 1949 at the Mescalero Hospital in Alamogordo, New Mexico at the age of 75.

Nanye-Hi (Nancy Ward, beloved Woman of the Cherokee) was born into the Cherokee Wolf clan circa 1738. In 1755, she stood by her husband during a fight against the Creeks, chewing the lead for bullets in order to provide his ammunition with deadly ridges. When her husband was fatally shot, Nanye-hi grabbed a rifle, rallied her fellow fighters and entered the battle herself. With her on their side, the Cherokee won the day.

These actions led to Nanye-hi being named Ghighau (Beloved Woman) of the Cherokee, a powerful position whose duties included leading the Women's Council and sitting on the Council of Chiefs. Nanye-hi also took part in treaty talks (to the surprise of male colonists when they were on the other side of the bargaining table).

As the years progressed, some Cherokee wanted to fight the Europeans who continued to crowd into their land. But Nanye-hi, who likely realized the Cherokee couldn't win against the numerous and well-supplied colonists, thought the two sides needed to learn to live together (she practiced coexistence herself, marrying an Englishman, Bryant Ward, in the late 1750s, which led to her being known as Nancy Ward). At a 1781 treaty conference, Nanye-hi declared, "Our cry is all for peace; let it continue. This peace must last forever."

Seeking peace didn't stop Nanye-hi from recognizing the dangers of ceding Cherokee territory — in 1817, she made an unsuccessful plea not to give up more land. When she died in 1822, she'd spent years trying to help her people acclimate to a changing world.

Brushing-Against and Little-Squint-Eyes, were the two San Carlos Apache women. The role of Native American women in their tribal societies differed from tribe to tribe, and was, in some cases, the polar opposite of the European culture which the settlers brought with them. For example, in the Iroquois Confederacy (People of the Longhouse) women were heads of their tribes. They appointed men to political positions, and removed them if they didn't fulfill their duties. When Europeans first encountered them, they asked to see the head chieftain, which caused a lot of confusion as the Iroquois didn't have male leaders. On the other side of the continent, in the Comancheria, the Comanche women skinned and harvested bison, took care of children, and had other duties which were more similar to the Europeans. Native American heritage was matrilineal, meaning one's heritage was tracked from their mother's side.

Chief Jackson Sundown, a nephew of Chief Joseph, was with him on the flight of the Nez Perce in 1877. He was the first native American to win a World Championship Bronc Rider title in 1916, at the age of 53, more than twice the age of the other competitors who made it to the final round. He is also the oldest person to ever win a rodeo world championship title. He was posthumously inducted into the Pendleton Round-Up Hall of Fame in 1972, into the National Cowboys of Color Museum and Hall of Fame in 1983, and the American Indian Athletes Hall of Fame in 1994.

Historical accounts of his life cite that Sundown, at a young age, displayed the traits of an athlete, riding his Appaloosa pony from the time he could walk. At age 14, his knack for handling horses earned him the privilege of caring for his tribes' horses and herding them when they moved camp during the turbulent 1877 Nez Perce War. On Aug. 9, 1877, the daring young Sundown displayed his stealth when his people were ambushed by the forces of the U.S. cavalry at Big Hole in southwestern Montana territory where they suffered many casualties, including women and children. Waaya-Tonah-Toesits-Kahn, although badly burned, outwitted the enemy and survived by hiding under a buffalo robe after they had torched his mother's teepee where he had been sleeping. Another legendary account of Sundown's bravery was when the Nez Perce, en route to Sitting Bulls camp in Canada, stopped to rest near Snake Creek in the Bear Paw Mountains just 40 miles south of the Canadian border. Unbeknownst to the Nez Perce, Brigadier General Nelson H. Miles had been dispatched to find and intercept them. Combined U.S. forces made an early morning surprise attack on the Nez Perce and after a three-day stand-off, the war weary Chief Joseph surrendered and declared he would "fight no more forever." Sundown, again displaying his prowess as a renegade Nez Perce warrior, escaped, although being wounded, "by clinging to the side of his horse so that it appeared riderless." Despite having no blankets or food, he and a small band of survivors made their way to Sitting Bull's camp in Canada.

Sundown is said to have lived in hiding with Sitting Bull and those that defeated General George Custer at the Battle of Little Big Horn as a war criminal for two years.

White Buffalo (Cheyenne) was born in 1862 &died in June 1929.He was described in newspaper articles in 1902 as being of striking appearance, as his hair had turned completely white when he was very young. His photo from his Carlisle days, dressed in a suit with a short haircut in the white man's style, shows that to be true. In 1888, when he was 26, he married a full-blood Northern Cheyenne widow. Medicine Woman, who was 30 at the time. She had also been born in Montana as had her parents. On the 1905 Indian Census for their reservation, they had four children listed: Emma White Buffalo, son Receiving Roots, Paul White Buffalo and Pratt White Buffalo - named for the Carlisle School founder. On the 1910 U. S. Federal Census, they are listed with only three of seven surviving children: John White Buffalo, James White Buffalo and Fred White Buffalo. According to the 1910 census, the mother of Medicine Woman also lived with them as well, 76 at the time, widowed and named Siege Woman. Medicine Woman is listed on this census as illiterate, as is her mother. His son, John White Buffalo enlisted for service in World War I. As full blood Cheyenne, both White Buffalo and Medicine Woman received land allotments on the reservation in 1891 in Lincoln Township in present-day Blaine County, Oklahoma. These are listed on several of the Indian Census lists as allotments number 966 and 967. White Buffalo lived to be 67 years old, and passed away on June 23, 1929, per the 1930 Indian census for the reservation. According to his obituary in the Watonga Republican newspaper dated June 27, 1929, he is buried at the Indian Mission Church on the reservation and was survived by his wife and sons.

Floyd Red Crow Westerman reached a mass international audience as the wise, old Sioux chief Ten Bears in Dances with Wolves (1990); he played the recurring role of the codebreaker Albert Hosteen on The X-Files (199599) and served as Indian chiefs, elders and shamans in dozens of other films and TV programs.

His deeply etched features personified the history of an entire people for western audiences. He was described by his friend Dennis Banks, the founder in 1968 of the American Indian Movement (AIM), as "the greatest cultural ambassador that Indian America ever had" and by Indian Country Today newspaper as "one of the most recognizable American Indians of the 20th century".

Comanche Marriage - When a man and a woman became joined in a good marriage, the majority of such relationships happened within Comanche bands. If it was found out that any such marriage between people who were related as kin, the union was completely forbidden.

When a young man took his wife into his tipi, the couple lived together near the parents. As a continued practice, a couple would reside in the same band right along with their parents.

In Comanche families with more than one wife in the household at one time, the Comanche elder Nemaruibetsi shared that the women did not request their husbands to gather additional wives. She added that in the old and past Comanche lifestyle, women outnumbered the men. The reason was that war had taken the lives of many men from the community.

In such a family with several wives and one husband, Nemaruibetsi told the tale of a favorite wife. The wife who was favored was normally the first married. A favored spouse made her own clothes but hardly did any work. The favorite wife did not have to cook or even carry water.

In addition, she noted that a man who married a number of sisters was viewed with more respect by others. The wives who were related to one another were generally friendly and created few disturbances in the family. However, if the wives were not related to one another, arguments and fights often ensued. With unrelated wives, Nemaruibetsi maintained the relationships were "dog-eat-dog".

Splendid standing portrait picture entitled "Utah, mother of the late Roe Kahrahrah", circa 1890-1910. The graceful Comanche woman is shown attired in a fine dress with a floral shawl encircling her waist. Utah was born in 1878. She was the wife of Nathan Kahrahrah who was born in 1877. When Utah passed away in 1927, she was buried at the Little Washita Cemetery near Fletcher, Oklahoma. Photograph courtesy of the Denver Public Library Special Collections, Denver, Colorado.

Of Bison and Humans - I am the largest land animal in North America and my picture often symbolizes the American West during the time of settlers, wagon trains, Cowboys and Indians, and you will even see my image on some of your money.

You likely know me as the American Buffalo, although in technical terms some of you refer to me as Bison. By what name I am known to you is not as important as the role we have played throughout life history.

When the explorer Columbus landed on Turtle Island in the late 1400's, my family population was estimated at nearly 60,000,000 and our home range was the majority of what is now called the United States, with some of our Wood Bison cousins living in the area of Canada. By 1890, our estimated population was around one thousand as we neared total extinction from being hunted by settlers, and slaughtered by others to starve out the 'Indians'.

Although some of your ancestors of that time raised concerns about this slaughter, nothing was actually done to bring it to an end as the government encouraged this killing to meet their goal of containing the Plains Indians. Sadly, this apathy among your kind continues to this day as cattle ranchers have taken land once ours to range their cattle for profit. This may not raise alarm with some of you concerning us, but consider that the greatest slaughter of my family took place between 1850 and 1890, and if we were to be killed at the rate of 1000 per day, it would take 164 of your years to complete this cycle, and yet, humans were able to achieve this in less than 40 years. This gives you an idea of what my family endured at the hands of humans.

This demonstrates the mindset of those whose life quest was based on greed for land and genocide of a native people; those who lived in harmony with their surroundings knowing that how they treated the earth and her inhabitants would come back full circle to their way of life.

Native Americans had great respect for my family members and took what they needed without killing an entire herd. We were honored with song and dance and our spirits were respected with the ensuing hunt. Our numbers were not greatly affected by their hunting as we were prolific and maintained our ability to do our part in keeping the natural world in balance.

There are many things you can learn about yourself from my family as we all share this small planet together. Native People looked to nature for lessons, warmth and livelihood and realized that all natural things are teachers and speak to us if only we take time to listen.

The males in my family can grow to around 2000 pounds and nearly 6 feet high at the shoulders, and although we may seem to be slow and cumbersome, we can run to speeds of 35 miles per hour. This is good to remember when meeting others of your species so that you don't assume one thing about that person when something entirely different may be the case. When we graze, we continue to move so we do not lay waste to the land and our hooves loosen the earth as we walk, run, or wallow which in turn makes it easier for grasses to grow and critters to dig. This is a reminder to you that there will be times you must move quickly and times to move more at ease, but whatever your pace, be considerate of what you are doing to our Earth Mother and not destroy or disrespect what is around you.

Our great strength is needed to walk this journey we have been given and will teach you that there will be times in your own life that you will need great strength to continue on your path and reach your goals. When the snow is heavy and food is scarce, we will use our massive heads to push snow aside and find grasses lying underneath. Keep in mind that as we do this, so you also can use your head in stressful situations rather than giving in to panic. Look at the whole situation, use your head (emotions don't move snow very well) and keep going until you resolve the situation or find the grass you are looking for. The cold winds of change will figuratively blow through your life from time to time and emotional winters can be endured with the right type of insulation. Our heavy winter hair is a reminder to you of this and just as you see us shed this heavy coat in the spring, so you are reminded that there will come the day you can shed the concerns you had during that winter time that settled upon your path.

Native Americans wasted nothing we had to offer. Our bones were tools and weapons, our hides clothing and shelter, our bladders water and boiling bags, and even our tails made good fly swatters. They understood, and many still understand, that taking a life is a serious thing and when this must be done, honor should be a large part of the process leaving little to zero waste. Here I would ask you humans to think about how much waste is created on your earth walk as you eat and build homes, buy new things or just get tired of what you have had for a time. Settlers and hunters were known to kill us, take our tongues and hides and leave the rest to rot on the plains. Waste created by greed and lack of respect. We Buffalo had no need for landfills nor did we bury toxic waste beneath the skin of our Earth Mother. All worked in a beautiful cycle from our birth to our fertilizing the ground in our death and in feeding other.

The Sacred Bear-Spear - Many generations ago, even before the Blackfeet used horses as beasts of burden, the tribe was undertaking its autumn migration, when one evening before striking camp for the night it was reported that a dog-sledge or cart belonging to the chief was missing.

To make matters worse, the chief's ermine robe and his wife's buckskin dress, with her sacred elk-skin robe, had been packed in the little cart.

Strangely enough, no one could recollect having noticed the dog during the march.

Messengers were dispatched to the camping-site of the night before, but to no avail.

At last the chief's son, Sokumapi, a boy about twelve years of age, begged to be allowed to search for the missing dog, a proposal to which his father, after some demur, consented.

Sokumapi set out alone for the last camping-ground, which was under the shadows of the Rocky Mountains, and carefully examined the site.

Soon he found a single dog-sledge track leading into a deep gulch, near the entrance to which he discovered a large cave.

A heap of freshly turned earth stood in front of the cave, beside which was the missing cart.

As he stood looking at it, wondering what had become of the dog which had drawn it, an immense grizzly-bear suddenly dashed out.

So rapid was its attack that Sokumapi had no chance either to defend himself or to take refuge in flight.

The bear, giving vent to the most terrific roars, dragged him into the cave, hugging him with such force that he fainted.

When he regained consciousness it was to find the bear's great head within a foot of his own, and he thought that he saw a kindly and almost human expression in its big brown eyes.

For a long time he lay still, until at last, to his intense surprise, the Bear broke the silence by addressing him in human speech.
"Have no fear," said the grizzly.

"I am the Great Bear, and my power is extensive.

I know the circumstances of your search, and I have drawn you to this cavern because I desired to assist you.

Winter is upon us, and you had better remain with me during the cold season, in the course of which I will reveal to you the secret of my supernatural power."

It will be observed that the circumstances of this tale are almost identical with those which relate to the manner in which the Beaver Medicine was revealed to mankind.

The hero of both stories remains during the winter with the animal, the chief of its species, who in the period of hibernation instructs him in certain potent mysteries.

The Bear, having reassured Sokumapi, showed him how to transform various substances into food.

His strange host slept during most of the winter; but when the warm winds of spring returned and the snows melted from the hills the grizzly became restless, and told Sokumapi that it was time to leave the cave.

Before they quitted it, however, he taught the lad the secret of his supernatural power.

Among other things, he showed him how to make a Bear-spear.

He instructed him to take a long stick, to one end of which he must secure a sharp point, to symbolize the bear's tusks.

To the staff must be attached a bear's nose and teeth, while the rest of the spear was to be covered with bear's skin, painted the sacred color, red.

The Bear also told him to decorate the handle with eagle's feathers and grizzly claws, and in

war-time to wear a grizzly claw in his hair, so that the strength of the Great Bear might go with him in battle, and to imitate the noise a grizzly makes when it charges.

The Bear furthermore instructed him what songs should be used in order to heal the sick, and how to paint his face and body so that he would be invulnerable in battle, and, lastly, told him of the sacred nature of the spear, which was only to be employed in warfare and for curing disease.

Thus if a person was sick unto death, and a relative purchased the Bearspear, its supernatural power would restore the ailing man to health.

Equipped with this knowledge, Sokumapi returned to his people, who had long mourned him as dead.

After a feast had been given to celebrate his home-coming he began to manufacture the Bear-spear as directed by his friend.

Shortly after his return the Crows made war upon the Blackfeet, and on the meeting of the two tribes in battle Sokumapi appeared in front of his people carrying the Bear-spear on his back.

His face and body were painted as the Great Bear had instructed him, and he sang the battle-songs that the grizzly had taught him.

After these ceremonies he impetuously charged the enemy, followed by all his braves in a solid phalanx, and such was the efficacy of the Bear magic that the Crows immediately took to flight.

The victorious Blackfeet brought back Sokumapi to their camp in triumph, to the accompaniment of the Bear songs.

He was made a war-chief, and ever afterward the spear which he had used was regarded as the palladium of the Blackfoot Indians.

In the spring the Bear-spear is unrolled from its covering and produced when the first thunder is heard, and when the Bear begins to quit his winter quarters; but when the Bear returns to his den to hibernate the spear is once more rolled up and put away.

The greatest care is taken to protect it against injury.

It has a special guardian, and no woman is permitted to touch it.

While hosting a guest, if the man softly knocked out his pipe, it was a cue for the guest to leave. As opposed to giving an excuse, showing boredom, or fatigue, the message was delivered without a word. The visitor would then say something to close the conversation, and leave quietly.

1901: A large African-American family and extended family pose in front of a small wooden house in Oklahoma - You have noticed that everything an Indian does in a circle, and that is because the Power of the World always works in circles, and everything and everything tries to be round. In the old days all our power came to us from the sacred hoop of the nation and so long as the hoop was unbroken the people flourished. The flowering tree was the living center of the hoop, and the circle of the four quarters nourished it. The east gave peace and light, the south gave warmth, the west gave rain and the north. With its cold and mighty wind came strength and endurance. This knowledge came to us from the outer world with our religion. Everything the power of the world does is done in a circle. The sky is round and I have heard that the earth is round like a ball and so are all the stars. The wind, in its greatest power, whirls. Birds make their nests in circles, for theirs is the same religion as ours. The sun comes forth and goes down again in a circle. The moon does the same and both are round. Even the seasons form a great circle in their changing and always come back again to where they were. The life of a man is a circle from childhood to childhood, and so it is in everything where power moves. Our teepees were round like the nests of birds, and these were always set in a circle, the nation's hoop, a nest of many nests, where the Great Spirit meant for us to hatch our children.

Curley was a scout for Gen. George Custer, and watched the 1876 Battle at the Little Big Horn from a periphery. He was described as a "remorse, taciturn sort of fellow and disinclined to make friends, and rarely talks or pays much attention to anyone." He once said, "I spring from Crow earth and will never leave it. A teepee and food for my wife and child—grass for my ponies—and I go back to the ground of my fathers."

Tȟatȟáŋka Waŋžíla, also known as **Henry Oscar One Bull No 75** was a Lakota warrior best known for being the nephew and adopted son of Sitting Bull who fought at the Battle of the Little Bighorn.

One Bull was related to many great names. His mother was Sitting Bull's sister - Good Feather. His father was chief Makes Room and his brother was White Bull. One Bull was adopted by Sitting Bull at the age of four, who gifted him a pinto horse which quickly bonded with One Bull. The pony became the swiftest horse in the camp, envied by all. One Bull fought at the Battle of the Little Bighorn in 1876. After escorting his mother to safety, he joined the fight, killing several troopers in battle. One Bull joined his uncle and his brother in fleeing to Canada following the victory at Little Bighorn. During the murder of Sitting Bull, One Bull's pregnant wife, Red Whirlwind, was in Sitting Bull's cabin. After hearing the gunshots he rushed into the cabin, and managed to save his wife. Following the death of Sitting Bull, One Bull reported that all of his personal household goods and some of his horses were taken. He and his brother White Bull were significant contributors to Stanley Vestal's biography of their uncle.

This post is largely a repost of one of my earliest publications which was shown to a significantly smaller audience, since I didn't have nearly as much followers back then. I thought I should publish it again, as it's centered around a very important figure in Native American and American history

Chief "Two Gun White Calf" (1872-1934), also known as **John Two Guns** and John White Calf Two Guns, this Blackfoot chief provided one of the most readily recognizable images of a Native American in the world after an impression of his portrait appeared on a common coin, the Indian head nickel. Two Guns White Calf was born in 1872 near Fort Benton, Montana, son of White Calf, who was known as the last chief of the Pikuni Blackfoot. His visage was used along with those of John Big Tree (Seneca) and Iron Tail (Sioux) in James Earl Fraser's composite design for the nickel. After the coin's release around the turn of the century, Two Guns White Calf became a fixture at Glacier National Park, where he posed with tourists. He also acted as a publicity spokesman for the Northern Pacific Railroad, whose public relations staff came up with the name "Two Guns White Calf". After the death of White Calf in 1902 he became a tribal leader and he died of pneumonia in 1934 at the age of sixty-three. He was buried in a Catholic cemetery at Browning, Montana. The Great Northern Railroad, always interested in promoting tourism to its Glacier Park Hotels and passenger traffic on its trains, sought to encourage the idea that Two Guns was the model but Fraser sent to the Commissioner of Indian Affairs in 1931, a letter in which he denied ever having seen Two Guns. But Charles Bevard, an auctioneer who had come into possession of a number of Two Guns' personal effects which led him into extensive historical research on the subject, suspected that the US Government wanted Fraser to "discredit" Two Guns as a coin model because they were afraid of the great influence he had on the tribes. The Chief headed a secret organization known as the Mad Dog Society which was attempting to preserve Blackfoot Heritage. Traditional Indian dances such as the Sun Dance and the Ghost Dance, which had been banned, were again being performed after American Indians received blanket citizenship in 1924. Bevard believed that the US Government feared that Chief Two Guns, like his father, might again take the fierce Blackfoot warriors on the warpath in an attempt to regain their land.

Native Encampment - In the mid-1600's the Ojibwa east of Lake Superior began to move westward, and by the late 1770's, Ojibwa settlements circled Lake Superior. One of these settlements was located on the Kaministikwia

River. Eye-witness accounts of Fort William in the early 1800's usually mention a Native encampment east of the palisade. A painting dated 1805 shows clusters of dome-shaped wigwams huddled at the south-east corner of the Fort; illustrations from the Hudson's Bay Company period (after 1821) depict conical tepees and wigwams.

These habitations reflect the culture of a people continually adapting to their environment as they had for thousands of years. Ojibwa family groups moved through these woodlands around Lake Superior in a seasonal round that included fishing, hunting, and gathering, and trade gatherings with other Native groups. With the coming of the Europeans, many Ojibwa incorporated the demands of the fur trade: trapping fur-bearing animals, and more prolonged contact with trading posts to supply pelts and other services.

The Ojibwa inhabiting the western Lake Superior region were also known as the Saulteaux, or Chippewa, while to the north were the Cree. Probably both tribes were represented at Fort William during the Rendezvous when Natives from surrounding areas came to trade their furs and exchange their labor and produce for commodities available at the Indian Shop. While most Natives departed for their hunting grounds as summer ended, some stayed behind to participate in winter activities of the fort.

During the NWC period, there were probably about 150 Ojibwa living in the Kaministikwia district. A number of Ojibwa names appear quite regularly in the Fort William transaction records, probably the members of the Ojibwa community adjacent to the fort. It is probable that they based their operations at Fort William, but continued to undertake seasonal journeys and encampments for the purpose of harvesting maple sugar, wild rice, snaring rabbits, fishing, and hunting game. One of these expeditions might last weeks or even months, so the Ojibwa population at Fort William was constantly in flux.

In addition to their own activities, the Ojibwa at Fort William supported the operation of the post. Women worked in the kitchen and canoe sheds, as well as the farm, and received payment in the form of trade goods. Men might be engaged in hunting or fishing for the NWC, and any other service in labour or expertise that the company might require.

As producers, the Ojibwa were integral to the needs of the NWC at Fort William. The transaction records show the quantity of provisions and materials supplied to the post and its personnel: bark, wattap and spruce for canoe-building, snowshoes, moccasins, skins, maple sugar, berries, wild rice, and fresh game.

Flying Hawk's Narrative:

I was born four miles below where Rapid City now is, in 1852, about full moon in March. "My father was Black Fox and my mother's name was Iron Cedarwoman. "My father was a chief. In a fight with the Crows he was shot below the right eye with an arrow; it was so deep that it could not be pulled out, but had to be pushed through to the ear. "My tribe was the Ogalalla clan. Our family roamed on hunts for game and enemies all about through the country and to Canada. My father died when he was eighty years old. He had two wives and they were sisters. My mother was the youngest and had five children. The other wife had eight children, making thirteen in all. Kicking Bear was my full brother, and Chief Black Fox was my half brother and was named for our father. "When ten years old I was in my first battle on the Tongue River—Montana now. It was an Overland Train of covered wagons who had soldiers with them. The way it was started, the soldiers fired on the Indians, our tribe, only a few of us. We went to our friends and told them we had been fired on by the soldiers, and they surrounded the train and we had a fight with them. I do not know how many we killed of the soldiers, but they killed four of us. "After that we had a good many battles, but I did not take any scalps for a good while. I cannot tell how many I killed when a young man. "When I was twenty years old we went to the Crows and stole a lot of horses. The Crows discovered us and followed us all night. When daylight came we saw them behind us. I was the leader. We turned back to fight the Crows. I killed one and took his scalp and a field glass and a Crow necklace from him. We chased the others back a long way and then caught up with our own men again and went on. It was a very cold winter. There were twenty of us and each had four horses. We got them home all right and it was a good trip that time. We had a scalp dance when we got back. "We soon moved camp. One night the Piegans came and killed one of our people. We trailed them in the snow all night. At dawn we came up to them. One Piegan stopped. The others went on. We surrounded the one. He was a brave man. I started for him. He raised his gun to shoot when I was twenty feet away. I dropped to the ground and his bullet went over me; then I jumped on him and cut him through below the ribs and scalped him. We tied the scalp to a long pole. The women blacked their faces and we had a big dance over it. "The next day I started out again with some men and we ran into a Crow camp. We got into that camp by moonlight, but we got caught. They started to fire on us. We all ran into a deep gulch. We got out, but when it was day we saw them coming with a herd 'of horses, going back to the Crow camp. We got in front of them and hid in a hollow. When I looked out I saw they had Sioux horses which they had stolen from our camp. "A big Crow was ahead and the others were riding behind. I took a good aim at the big Crow and shot him in the chest. The rest of them left the horses and ran away. The big Crow was still living. I took another shot at him, then I took his scalp. We took all the horses they had stolen. There were sixty-nine head that time. "Some time after we went to hunt buffalo. All the men went on this hunt. While we were butchering the kill some Piegans were coming. We went to meet them and had a fight. Some missed their 'horses and were running on foot. I was on a good fast horse. I ran over one and knocked him down and fell on him and scalped him alive (ugh). Another one of my people was close by and he shot the one I scalped. This fight was below where Fort Peck is. "More Piegans came. More of them than us. We were attacked by the Piegans. I kneeled down beside a sage bush. A Piegan shot at me but missed. I shot at him and hit his horse. It went down. Then I turned back and ran into a Piegan. Four of them were butchering buffaloes. I shot at them but missed. The Piegans ran and left their horses, and I took them all. We killed three of the Piegans. They shot one of our horses through the head. The fight was over and the Piegans went to a hill. "On the way back we ran into a lot of Crows and we had a fight on horseback. We chased them but no one was killed.

Geraldine Keams (born August 19, 1951 in Flagstaff, Arizona) is an Navajo actress. She is best known for her work in numerous television series. Keams made her film debut playing Little Moonlight in Clint Eastwood's western, The Outlaw Josey Wales in 1976.

In addition to her film work, Keams gives live performances and workshops. She is a resident artist at the Los Angeles Music Center. Keam currently resides in Pasadena, California.

Rose Bompard (1911-1919) - The young Crow (Apsáalooke) woman wore a full-length dress decorated with elk ivories. Each elk had only two ivory teeth, vestigial tusks, so some might have been antler or bone reproductions. A single hole was made in each for attachment to the dress. (Click image to enlarge/clarify.) The several hundred ivories indicated a family of good hunters or enough wealth to acquire ivories.

Rose Bompard married Glen Bird in 1919. She died in 1978 at age 81. Richard Throssel captured the portrait on an 8x10 inch glass plate negative, either while living on the Crow Reservation in eastern Montana or in his studio at Billings if the date was after 1911. Throssel's work was largely ignored until the 1997 publication of "Crow Indian Photographer." -Gary Coffrin.

About to embark on the road of captivity and exile, the Chiricahua Apache women at Fort Bowie were changing women. They were the brave mothers, wives, daughters, widows, warriors, lovers, and friends of the Chiricahua men with whom General Crook met at Canyon de los Embudos. Some faced exile together with their beloved men, while many had only each other and their children for comfort, yet others children were taken. Battling nearly overwhelming obstacles, the women managed to care for themselves and their children until felled by a relentless tide of deadly diseases. These were the very real women of legend and lore, the grandmothers and greatgrandmothers of living Chiricahua Apaches for whom the Chiricahua men fought.

Standing Bear (ca. 1829–1908) The legal battle of Ponca Chief Standing Bear (Ma-chu-nah-zha) to remain in his homeland became a landmark civil rights case for American Indians. Standing Bear was born about 1829, probably in the Niobrara River Valley in present Nebraska. Little is known about his early life, but by the 1860s he had become a tribe leader. During the 1870s his people faced a desperate situation. Sandwiched between the expanding United States and the hostile Brule Lakota, the Ponca were removed by the federal government to the Indian Territory, present Oklahoma, in 1877.

The rigors and emotional trauma of their removal ravaged the Ponca. Perhaps as many as one-third of the tribe, including Standing Bear's son, soon perished. Wanting to bury his son in their ancestral homeland, Standing Bear and about thirty followers abandoned Indian Territory in January 1879. Captured by the army, they were incarcerated at Fort Omaha, Nebraska.

In late March and early April 1879 newspaper editor Thomas Henry Tibbles interviewed Standing Bear in detainment and published a story that grabbed the public's attention. Lawyers volunteered their services and filed a writ of habeas corpus to prevent Standing Bear and his people from being returned to Indian Territory. In Standing Bear v. Crook (1879), federal judge Elmer Dundy ruled in Standing Bear's favor, claiming that "an Indian is a person under the meaning of the law," and thus the federal government had no right to hold the Poncas.

Thereafter the tribe was divided. The majority Southern Ponca remained in Indian Territory. Standing Bear and his followers, however, returned to Nebraska and became the Northern Ponca. Standing Bear lived on an allotment until his death in September 1908. Dedicated in 1996, a twentytwo-foot-tall bronze statue of Standing Bear, by artist Oreland C. Joe, highlights the Chief Standing Bear Native American Memorial Park in Ponca City.

Chief Blue Horse was born in 1820; SHON-KEE-TOH. He witnessed the meeting of Chief Dull Knife; The Treaty of Fort Laramie was an agreement between the United States and the Lakota nation, signed in 1868 at Fort Laramie in the Wyoming Territory, guaranteeing to the Lakota ownership of the Black Hills, and further land and hunting rights in South Dakota, Wyoming, and Montana. The Powder River Country was to be henceforth closed to all whites. The treaty ended Red Cloud's War. The treaty included articles intended to "insure the civilisation" of the Lakota; financial incentives for them to farm land and become competitive - and stipulations that minors should be provided with an "English education" at a "mission building". To this end the US government included in the treaty that white teachers, blacksmiths and a farmer, a miller, a carpenter, an engineer and a government agent should take up residence within the reservation. Repeated violations of the otherwise exclusive rights to the land by gold prospectors led to the Black Hills War.

Indiana Poem:

Time is running out for me too,

And life has left scars on my face.

Though my body is growing old, My

soul will always stay young. The

day will come,

When I too will cross the bridge,

And leave this earthly life behind.

But as long as you remember me, I'll live in your heart.

My soul will stay with you,

You will see my face in the rising sun.

My eyes in the stars,

That look down on you every night.

I'll look back one last time,

And then my form will be slowly swallowed up on the other shore.

My own poem.

Medicine Crow and son, pose outside sitting on a wooden crate. She's wearing a dress decorated with elk teeth. Men with horses and a mother and daughter are in the background.

Yakama Woman - The Yakama are a federally recognized Washington State tribe, consisting of a federation including: Yakama, Klickitat, Walla Walla, Wanapum, Wenatchi, Palouse, and Wishram people. They number approximately 30,000.

Chief Iron Tail (Oglala Lakota: Siŋté Máza in Standard Lakota Orthography, 1842-May 29, 1916) was an Oglala Lakota Chief and a star performer with Buffalo Bill's Wild West. Iron Tail was one of the most famous Native American celebrities of the late 19th and early 20th centuries and a popular subject for professional photographers who circulated his image across the continents. Iron Tail is notable in American history for his distinctive profile on the Buffalo nickel or Indian Head nickel of 1913 to 1938.

Siŋté Máza was the chief's tribal name. Asked why the white people call him Iron Tail, he said that when he was a baby his mother saw a band of warriors chasing a herd of buffalo, in one of their periodic grand hunts, their tails standing upright as if shafts of steel, and she thereafter called his name Siŋté Máza as something new and novel.

Chief Iron Tail is often mistaken by historians for Chief Iron Hail ("Dewey Beard"), being Lakota contemporaries with similar sounding names. Most biographies incorrectly report that Chief Iron Tail fought in the Battle of the Little Bighorn and that his family was killed in 1890 at Wounded Knee, when in truth it was Chief Iron Hail who suffered the loss. Major Israel McCreight reported: "Iron Tail was not a war chief and no remarkable record as a fighter. He was not a medicine man or conjuror, but a wise counselor and diplomat, always dignified, quiet and never given to boasting. He seldom made a speech and cared nothing for gaudy regalia, very much like the famed War Chief Crazy Horse. In this respect he always had a smile and was fond of children, horses and friends."

Chief Iron Tail no 90 was an international personality and appeared as the lead with Buffalo Bill at the Champs-Élysées in Paris, France and the Colosseum In Rome, Italy. In France, as in England, Buffalo Bill and Iron Tail were feted by the aristocracy. Iron Tail was one of Buffalo Bill's best friends and they hunted elk and bighorn together on annual trips. On one of his visits to The Wigwam of Major Israel McCreight, Buffalo Bill asked Iron Tail to illustrate in pantomime how he played and won a game of poker with U S. army officials during a Treaty Council in the old days. "Going through all the forms of the game from dealing to antes and betting and drawing a last card during which no word was uttered and his countenance like a statue, he suddenly swept the table clean into his blanket and rose from the table and strutted away. It was a piece of superb acting, and exceedingly funny." Iron Tail continued to travel with Buffalo Bill until 1913, and then the Miller Brothers 101 Ranch Wild West until his death in 1916.

Buffalo Bill and Käsebier were similar in their abiding Native American culture and maintained friendships with the Sioux. Buffalo Bill quickly approved Käsebier's request and she began her project on Sunday morning, April 14, 1898. Käsebier's project was purely artistic and her images were not made for commercial purposes and never used in Buffalo Bill's Wild West program booklets or promotional posters.

Käsebier took classic photographs of the Sioux while they were relaxed. Chief Iron Tail was one of Käsebier's most challenging portrait subjects. Käsebier's session with Chief Iron Tail was her only recorded story:

"Preparing for their visit to Käsebier's photography studio, the Sioux at Buffalo Bill's Wild West Camp met to distribute their finest clothing and accessories to those chosen to be photographed." Käsebier admired their efforts, but desired to, in her own words, photograph a "real raw Indian, the kind I used to see when I was a child', referring to her early years in Colorado and on the Great Plains. Käsebier selected one Indian, Chief Iron Tail, to approach for a photograph without regalia. He did not object. The resulting photograph was exactly what Käsebier had envisioned: a relaxed, intimate, quiet, and beautiful portrait of the man, devoid of decoration and finery, presenting himself to her and the camera without barriers. Several days later, however, when presented with the photograph, Chief Iron Tail immediately tore up the image, stating it was too dark. Käsebier photographed him once again, this time in his full feather headdress, much to his satisfaction. Chief Iron Tail was an international celebrity. He appeared with his fine regalia as the lead with Buffalo Bill at the Avenue des Champs-Élysées in Paris, France, and the Colosseum of Rome. Chief Iron Tail was a superb showman and chaffed at the photo of him relaxed. But Käsebier chose it as the frontispiece for a 1901 Everybody's Magazine article. Käsebier believed all the portraits were a "revelation of Indian character," showing the strength and individual character of the Native Americans in "new phases for the Sioux."

Early in the twentieth century, Iron Tail's distinctive profile became well known across the United States as one of three models for the five-cent coin Buffalo nickel or Indian Head nickel. The popular coin was introduced in 1913 and showcases the native beauty of the American West. Bee Ho Gray, the famous Wild West performer, accompanied Chief Iron Tail to act as an interpreter and guide to Washington D.C. and New York where Iron Tail modeled for sculptor James Earle Fraser as he worked on designs for the new Buffalo nickel. Iron Tail was the most famous Native American of his day and a popular subject for professional photographers who circulated his image across the continents.

In May 1916 Chief Iron Tail, at the age of 74, became ill with pneumonia while performing with the Miller Brothers 101 Ranch Wild West in Philadelphia, Pennsylvania, and was placed in St. Luke's Hospital. Buffalo Bill was obliged to go on with his show next day to Baltimore, Maryland, and Iron Tail was left alone in a strange city with doctors and nurses who could not communicate with him. McCreight learned about the Chief's admission to the hospital in the morning Philadelphia paper, and immediately sent a telegram to Buffalo Bill to send Iron Tail by next train to Du Bois, Pennsylvania, for care at The Wigwam. No reply was had and the wire was not delivered or forwarded to Baltimore. Instead the hospital authorities put Chief Iron Tail on a Pullman, ticketed for home to the Black

Hills. On May 28, 1916, when the porter of his car went to wake him at South Bend, Indiana, Iron Tail was dead, his body continuing on to its destination. Buffalo Bill expressed regret that the Chief was sent to the hospital and that he had not received the telegram. Iron Tail's body was transferred to a hospital in Rushville, Nebraska, then to Pine Ridge Indian Reservation, where he was buried at Holy Rosary Mission Cemetery on June 3, 1916. With deep emotion, Buffalo Bill said he was going to put a granite stone on Chief Iron Tail's grave with a replica of the Buffalo nickel (for which Chief Iron Tail had posed) carved on it as a memento. However, Buffalo Bill died on January 10, 1917, just six months after Chief Iron Tail's death. In a ceremony at Buffalo Bill's grave on Lookout Mountain, west of Denver, Colorado, Chief Flying Hawk laid his war staff of eagle feathers on the grave. Each of the veteran Wild Westers placed a Buffalo nickel on the imposing stone as a symbol of the Indian, the buffalo, and the scout, figures since the 1880s that were symbolic of the early history of the American West.

Hash-Nash-Shut (a Wasco Indian chief, in the year 1906) was originally from the Confederated Tribes of Umatilla but married into the Confederated Tribes of Warm Springs. Before becoming the Confederated Tribes of Warm Springs in 1938, the three tribes; Wasco, Warm Springs, and Paiute, lived along the Columbia River and Cascade Mountains. They all spoke different languages and had their own customs.

The Warm Springs and Wasco bands gave up ownership rights to a 10,000,000-acre (40,000 km2) area, which they had inhabited for over 10,000 years, in exchange for basic health care, education, and other forms of assistance as outlined by the Treaty with the Tribes of Middle Oregon (June 25, 1855).

Apart from the Bald Eagle feathers in his hair, and white mink furs wrapped around his braids, Hash-Nash-Shut is wearing what seems to be a trade blanket. Trade blankets were initially manufactured for trade to native tribes in exchange for beaver furs and other goods at established trading posts throughout the Western United States and Canada. The period between 1880 and 1930 is considered the golden age of the Native American trade blanket. There were five American companies that dominated this market, with Pendleton Woolen Mills being the most famous. They are still in business to this day.

Trade Blankets - From the outset, Pendleton stood apart from other manufacturers, as it was established to deal solely with Native American trade and was the first company to utilize Native Americans as advisers in developing its designs. The Umatilla and Cayuse tribes were among Pendleton's initial customers, and for this reason, Pendleton originally set up shop on the Old Umatilla Reservation in Oregon.

Although the earliest of these blankets were very basic, incorporating only blocks, rectangles and crosses, the introduction of the Jacquard loom in the early 1900's revolutionized the industry and allowed for much more intricate designs and the characteristic zigzag patterns.

With this knowledge, we can assume Hash-Nash-Shut's blanket with its rectangular pattern was one of the earlier designs.

Bull Chief (born in 1825, Died February 4th 1914) was part of the Crow, or Apsaroke tribe. He was interviewed by a man named Edward S. Curtis, who visited many tribes during the 20th century for interviews and to take portraits of the Natives. As a young man Bull Chief was never very successful when he was part of war-parties and always returned home without honor. He believed it was unnecessary for one to fast in order to be successful in a battle, and therefore opted not to fast. Being so unsuccessful after returning from battle after battle, Bull Chief decided to climb Cloud Peak, which is the highest peak of the Bullhorn Mountains in Wyoming. Bull Chief stayed up on Cloud Peak for one day and one night hoping to have a vision, but having no luck he had to leave because mountain-rats were biting through his clothes and a fierce blizzard was causing hazardous conditions. When Bull Chief returned home, his village was getting ready to be moved to a new location. Based on landmarks mentioned in the new location, it appears the tribe was moved near Red Lodge Creek, MT. During this transition time, Bull Chief decided to continue trying to fast in order to have a vision. He fasted for four days and four nights, but still had no vision. After which, he tried two more times unsuccessfully. Seeing that his current attempts were failing, and all of the other men in his tribe counting coup he again decided to try something new. For this attempt, he went up to the head of Red Lodge Creek to fast for four days and for four nights in blinding snow. This time his experience turned out much different from all of his previous attempts. He had a vision in which he, "Saw his own lodge and a splendid bay horse standing in front of it." It was not explained as to what this vision meant, but thereafter Bull Chief began to do remarkably well in battles. Shortly after the vision, Bull Chief was able to get his first honor and started counting coupe frequently. Counting coup is the highest honor for winning intertribal wars between

Plains Indians. Bull Chief's determination and personal strength helped him to his successes as a hunter, in combat, and in spiritual pursuits.

Bull Chief was a fierce warrior who led his warriors into battle against the United States Army in the Great Plains, raiding white settlements during the course of the 1870s, operating in Apsaroke territory to help his people survive against the westward expansion. But after the wars were over, he moved to the Crow Reservation. In 1908, he met photographer Edward S. Curtis and had his picture taken, an elderly veteran whose war years were long past.

Bull Chief took 15 wives in total and gave up 13 of them. One of Bull Chief's wives, most likely his first because she is referred to as his young wife, was killed by a bank of earth falling on her. In order to mourn for his young wife, Bull Chief decided he wanted to go through some form of torture to honor her death. Shortly after he made his decision to endure torture for his wife, two local tribesmen went out and killed a buffalo bull and brought back the head attached to a long strip of skin and including the tail at the end, to the edge of the village When Bull Chief heard of this, the next morning he went out and bathed; afterward, he went to Big Shadow, a clansman, to ask him to pierce him. Big Shadow accepted and instructed Bull Chief to go bathe again, remove every ornament from his body, rub himself with sage, and he would come and meet him.

After Bull Chief had concluded his tasks, Big Shadow came and found him, bringing with him three other men. Big Shadow started off the process then by painted Bull Chief from head to toe with white clay. Once Bull Chief was painted, Big Shadow then pierced Bull Chief's back muscle in two separate places and thrust skewers through the slits in his muscle to attach the thongs fastened to the nostrils of the buffalo head. Next Big Shadow pierced Bull Chief's shoulders and from those slits, hung the shield and tomahawks. Bull Chief was then given a staff and instructed to get up off the ground. After getting up Big Shadow told Bull Chief he needed to walk around the village four times while the three men with them would smoke. This was a difficult task for Bull Chief to accomplish, because the dogs in the community would jump on the skin and when dogs were not jumping on it, it was getting caught in the sage brush under it.

At sunset Bull Chief went up on a hilltop and laid down with his head between the horns of the buffalo and his feet at the tail, pointing east. He stayed up on the hilltop all night to rest from the day's activities. During his sleep, Bull Chief had another vision, this time of a man standing at his feet, then turning and departing Big Shadow came up on the hilltop around sunrise and informed Bull Chief that he knew someone had come and visited him the night before. At first Bull Chief did not tell Big Shadow what the man looked like who had visited him, but after Bull Chief bathed and cleaned up he joined Big Shadow again and then told him about the man. The description Bull Chief gave Big Shadow of the man led Big Shadow to believe this man was his father, Morning Star.

Iron Eagle was considered the greatest War Chief of the Cheyenne. He fought many battles, always winning.

He was not afraid of any other man or Tribe. His courage was legendary and he and his horse, always the fastest, were the pride of his Tribe.

One day Iron Eagle's brother, Four Fingers, came to tell him that Spotted Fawn, the most beautiful woman in the Tribe had agreed that he also wanted to marry Spotted Fawn. But Four Fingers knew he did not stand a chance. He was not a great warrior, because he was crippled.

As a small boy he had lost both his thumbs in an accident so. his name. Without a grip, he was unable to throw a spear or hold a knife as well as others. Never would he have a beautiful woman or win a war like Iron Eagle. His only consolation was that the people considered him special because four was a sacred number.

There were four seasons, four directions, and four names for Spirit, and this man had only four fingers; that was a special sign. Iron Eagle was very happy with the news of Spotted Fawn. To celebrate, he declared that he and a group of warriors would attack their age-old enemies, the Arapaho.
Iron Eagle gathered the warriors together and set out the next day, telling Spotted Fawn he would bring her a victory for a wedding present. It would be his greatest victory. But Spotted Fawn could not stand to see him go off to war alone, so she dressed like a warrior and rode out with the war party. She would not let him fight alone. The only one who recognized her was Four Fingers. The battle turned out to be a very difficult one for the Cheyenne. They were greatly outnumbered by the Arapaho, but Iron Eagle still felt he could win.

Then, suddenly, he noticed a strange thing. One of his warriors, who had been fatally struck by an arrow, fell from his horse and long, black hair fell from the headband. The warrior was a woman. Then Iron Eagle realized it was Spotted, Fawn. She was dead, killed by the Arapaho Chief.

Everyone seemed to realize at once what had happened. All the warriors stopped fighting, for they realized that a woman had been killed. Both sides stopped and there was silence on the battlefield. Then Iron Eagle, in revenge, sped for the Arapaho Chief.

He would get revenge for the death of this woman. But the Arapaho Chief made a deceptive move and evaded Iron Eagle and stabbed him.

Then the Arapaho Chief raised his spear over Iron Eagle and Spotted Fawn and the Cheyenne began to run. Their great Chief had been killed. Then out of the running pack came Four Fingers. He rode straight for all the Arapaho, who were lined up ready to kill the retreating Cheyenne. One man against all the Arapaho; they couldn't believe it. And when Four Fingers raised his hands in the air, all could see he had no weapons.

The Arapaho Chief sat on his horse, hypnotized by the lone warrior who would challenge the Arapaho without a weapon. Then Four Fingers knocked the Arapaho Chief off his horse and jumped on him. Four Fingers reached out with a deformed hand and touched the Arapaho Chief. He did not hurt him. He stood up, facing the Arapaho, and raised a hand straight up in front of the chief with his four fingers raised and said, "How" which means "Peace".

The Arapaho saw that he had only four fingers and they knew he was a holy man. Because of his courage, they answered him in return with "How". Since that time the Arapaho and the Cheyenne have never fought one another. And the four-finger peace sign became a sign used by all the people. And during battles, it became common practice for warriors to touch one another to show courage instead of killing each other.

The **"Cherokee Kid"** was a stage name for Will Rogers. William Penn Adair Rogers was born on November 4, 1879 on a ranch near Oologah, Indian Territory (now Oklahoma) to a respected mixed-blood Cherokee couple. In 1898, he left his family's ranch to work as a Texas cowboy, then traveled to Argentina, where he was a gaucho. One particular talent was discovered in 1902, when he joined Texas Jack's Wild West Show as a trick roper and rider under the stage name "The Cherokee Kid." He was so good, he won a spot in the Guinness Book of World Records for throwing three lassos at once—the first went around the horse's neck, the second around the rider, and the last under the horse to loop all four legs together.

Death in the Tribe - Losing a child and having to bury them. A man lost his son and couldn't bare the thought of living without him. He was suffering and couldn't believe his son was gone. He cried and cried every day and night, missing his son, wishing things were different.

He couldn't sleep and hadn't slept in a long time. One night an old medicine man came to him in a dream and told him "Enough!! That's enough crying!!" The dad told him "I cannot stop, I am never going to see him again!" The old Medicine man said, "Do you want to see him again?" The dad says "yes of course" the old medicine man takes him to the entrance of happy hunting ground where he sees many little beautiful children, so happy and innocent, carrying eagle feathers into the happy hunting grounds, smiling and laughing and just so beautiful. The dad asks "where is my son? Who are these kids?" The old medicine man said "these are the children that are called home early, they are innocent and loved and they go right through to the happy hunting grounds, so happy" the dad says "and my son? Where is he? Why isn't he with these children?" The old medicine man said, "come this way" and guided him to the side of entrance. A small boy with a beautiful smile was standing there watching all the children enter the happy hunting grounds. He was standing there within reach of an eagle's feather. His dad grabbed him and hugged him, and the boy kissed his dads' cheeks and told him he missed him. The dad said "why don't you have a eagles feather like the other kids? Why are you waiting here at the entrance?" The boy said "I keep trying to get the eagle feather Daddy, but your tears pull it out of reach. I see you are so sad, and I am tied to that feeling so I wait here until you're ok" the dad burst out crying for the last time, he told his son, "Get that eagle feather and go, I will be ok, and I know you will be too."

- Don't cry too long for that loved one you lost, whether son, daughter, husband, mother or father!! Let them rest in peace, don't torment your life, because they won't come back, have faith that you will be together again, and that Creator makes us a beautiful home with all our loved ones when we leave this world.

Dog Travois - Travois were hauled by dogs before horses started appearing on the Northern Plains by the late 1600s. Horses, named "elk dogs" or "big dogs" by some tribes, could carry more weight, thus allowing larger tipis for nomadic tribes. Horses also revolutionized hunting and warfare techniques.

The elderly woman, perhaps a Lakota Sioux named Red Thunder, reportedly held the staff of her husband, Little Bull, and posed in her best regalia. A finely-crafted miniature buffalo was on the dog's back found at the Buffalo Bill Museum.

"The animals want to communicate with man, but Wakan-Tanka does not intend they shall do so directly, man must do the greater part in securing an understanding". --Brave Buffalo, Teton Sioux.

Chief Thunderhawk (Cetan Wakiyan) - Though little is written about Chief Thunderhawk, it is known that as a young man he was a companion of Sitting Bull, and a warrior of prominence. Since the Hunkpapa were a small band, Thunderhawk figured was important in Hunkpapa and Lakota affairs. He was chief of his band, a position which he retained all his life. His band followed the buffalo.

According to the **Comanche Elder Herman Asenap,** any disputes among people in the village were handled by band leaders. Within the band, he shared that the members had one Chief and his helpers. If a Chief became old, his role of Chief could be turned over to a younger warrior.

Also, Herman noted that marriages were either made between members of the various Comanche bands or from within their own band. Marriage was definitely not allowed between blood relatives. If any such kin were found out, the two people were then separated from one another.

On his own, a young Comanche could eagerly try to seek the consent of a girl's father in order to wed his daughter. In the days of older Comanche life, Herman maintained that the girls generally did not marry before seventeen or eighteen years of age. If a young suitor was successful and married the young lady, the new son-in-law had some new responsibilities favoring his father-in-law. When the two men were together, the son-in-law did all of the work for his new father-in-law.

Indian Territory. Circa 1890-1895. Photograph courtesy of the Missouri History Museum, Saint Louis, Missouri.

The well-known **Comanche Elder Post Oak Jim (Tahkahper)** was born in1865 and passed away in 1950.

In his long life, Post Oak was known as an excellent singer of Comanche songs, a storied dancer, a peyote leader, and a very fine horseman.

As a youngster, he had arrived at the KCA reservation with other Comanches. From the 1880's onward, tribal members recalled Post Oak Jim as a man of strength. As a cattleman and farmer, Jim lived in his home located around a half-mile west of Cache Creek. He was a cousin to Topay. Topay was the last surviving wife of Chief Quanah Parker.

The Texas born Knox Beal, who served as an Indian Agency interpreter, shared the following about Post Oak Jim:

"In the young days, he was quite a horseman. Many times he has held wild horses for me while I got on. He would ride them with ease." Knox added "He was liked by all and everyone who knew him."

Even though Post Oak Jim lived the final three years of his long life in blindness at his home, he still faced life with much courage.

Jim had worked as a tribal policeman at the sub-Indian Agency in Cache, Oklahoma, he nearly lived all year in his teepee. Courtesy of the Fort Worth Star-Telegram, Fort Worth, Texas. Additional information from the Lawton Morning Press, Times Record News, Wichita Falls, Texas, and the Fort Worth Star-Telegram.

Wakinyan Ohank'o (1839-1914) Fast Thunder - I've read and heard a lot about grandpa Fast Thunder over these past few years. He counted coup several times and gave accounts of each time. He pierced many dancers at the Mniconjou Sun Dance in 1877 held below Spotted Tail agency to honor Crazy Horse. He went to Washington DC 4 times to advocate on behalf of our Lakota Oyate.

At the request of Old Man Afraid of his Horse he became head security at Pine Ridge agency society named Wiciska. He was a yuwipi man that helped Crazy Horse and his warrior society with medicine to win in battle.

He grew medicines and knew where to pick them, he was called upon to heal the sick in the community before there were doctors or IHS.

It was told he was given Crazy Horses medicine bundle to look after, which he passed on to his daughter and son in law. George Means and Fannie Fast Thunder.

My grandma told me he stitched up wounded and near dying that made it to his home between Wounded Knee and Manderson the night of the Wounded Knee massacre. Some even stayed with him there for some time after.

He was said to have the brand 707 because he raised that many head of horses.

He also served as tribal judge for some years.

My grandma Estella King/Apples mother was named Stella Fast Thunder/King, her dad is Fast Thunder. This is how I am a descendent.

William Bald Eagle (April Eagle, 8, 1919 – July 22, 2016), also known as Chief David Beautiful Bald David was a Lakota actor, soldier, stuntman, and musician.

Dave Bald Eagle was born in a tipi on the west banks of Cherry Creek, on the Cheyenne River Sioux Tribe Reservation in South Dakota.

Bald Eagle first enlisted in the Fourth Cavalry of the United States Army and served out his enlistment. During World War II, he re-enlisted in the 82nd Airborne Division ("All American Division") where he fought in the Battle of Anzio, being awarded a Silver Star, and in the D-Day invasion of Normandy at which time he received a Purple Heart Medal when he was wounded.

After the Second World War, Bald Eagle worked in a number of occupations including drummer, race car driver, semi-pro baseball player, and rodeo performer before beginning a career in Hollywood films. He was the grandson of famous Lakota warrior White Bull!

During the last decade prior to the establishment of reservations, the **Omaha Dance** had achieved prominence as a successful celebration for petitioning supernatural protection in warfare activities. The dance was the property of the Omaha society, a man's organization. Accordingly, participation was restricted to society members and their families. Certain sacred badges of distinction were reserved for outstanding members. Prominent features of the celebration included dancing, oratory, give-aways, ritual drama, and feasting. The song, oratory, and dance pantomine aroused a patriotic fervor while warfare achievements and victories were reenacted. Giveaways, public distributions of gifts by hosts and other prominent persons, served to reinforce social relationships and demonstrate generosity. All ceremonies climaxed with a ritual drama or kettle dance, which included a flamboyant display of dancing with warriors dramatically vanquishing the enemy, symbolized by a pail of cooked dog meat. Typically, celebrations also served as protracted social affairs, and lasted well into the night.

Cheyenne Sun Dance (c.1903) - Every summer after renewal of the sacred arrow, Cheyenne people prayed for protection and prosperity, in a ritual called the 'sun dance'. With elaborate paint schemes on their bodies, participating men danced and fasted for 4 consecutive days.

The Grass Dance is one of the oldest-known tribal dances. Dancers perform this to pay respects to departed ancestors and to ask Mother Earth for strength.

Wounded Knee (1890) - In the late 1880s, the Paiute Shaman Wovoka gave the American Indians of the Great Plains some much needed hope. He taught that the traditional ways of the Native Americans could return. The spirits of the dead would return, the buffalo would come back and a tidal wave of soil would bury the whites and restore the prairie. In order to bring these events to pass, dancers needed to dance the Ghost Dance. The dancers would wear brightly colored shirts decorated with eagles and buffalos. The ghost shirts would protect the wearer from the bullets of the soldiers. Sitting Bull encouraged *the Ghost Dance religion*.

By 1890 white settlers and the Indian agents in charge of overseeing the reservation were fearful of the encouraged Native Americans. General Nelson A. Miles assembled an army of over 5,000 to contain the bands in the area. The government ordered the chiefs arrested. While attempting to arrest Sitting Bull, troops killed the famous Lakota chief.

Upon hearing about the death of Sitting Bull, **Chief Big Foot** and approximately 300 of his band headed south, seeking the protection of the Pine Ridge Reservation. Col. James W. Forsyth and his troops intercepted the group at Wounded Knee Creek. On the morning of December 29, 1890 Big Foot and his warriors were meeting with the Army officers. A shot rang out. The soldiers turned their rifles on the Native Americans. From the heights above, rapid-firing Hotchkiss guns were fired at the encampment. As the men, women and children fled, some into the ravine next to the camp, they were cut down in a cross-fire. Those not suffering that fate were chased by the soldiers and butchered. In all over 153 Sioux men women and children were massacred, 44 were wounded. Big Foot was among the dead.

The massacre effectively ended the *Ghost Dance movement* and was the last large encounter of the Indian Wars.

Mary Louise Defender-Wilson was born near the rural town of Shields, North Dakota, where she now lives on the Standing Rock (Sioux) Indian Reservation. She is primarily Dakotah Sioux, though a grandmother was Hidatsa. Her tribal name is Wagmuhawin -- Gourd Woman.

Defender-Wilson was born into a family of storytellers. The first story she remembers hearing was the tale of how the Dakotah culture hero Stone Boy was tricked out of his fancy clothes by Unktomi (Spider Man), a trickster figure. By the time she was in fifth grade, she was telling stories to her classmates. "Sometimes I got off the beaten path, but everyone laughed, especially at the Spider Man stories," she recalled.

The stories taught that people came to Earth in animal form and had a lot to learn in order to live in harmony with others. Many stories also related to the land. "We lived by gardening and as sheep herders," she said. "We would follow along with the Old Ones and the dogs who tended the sheep. We could walk all over the land. There were no fences, and Grandfather would tell us about the rock formations, hills, streams and buttes we came across." Double Woman Hill west of Shields, for instance, takes its name from a mythical being who appears in dreams and is linked to artistry, design, and industriousness.

Defender-Wilson's personal story is as compelling as the traditional tales she tells. A tall, physically attractive woman, she was once named Miss Indian America. She held administrative jobs with Indian-related government agencies and struggled with the issue of her identity. In 1976, she returned to the reservation, having realized that forcing herself to assimilate into white culture would be a form of suicide. For several years in the 1980s, she taught tribal culture and language at Fort Yates Community College. She has taught Dakotah storytelling through the North Dakota Council on the Arts Traditional Arts Apprenticeship Program, given lecture demonstrations throughout the region and educated teachers in DakotahHidatsa storytelling and culture. She has produced a radio program to teach the Siouan language and to promote the intellectual value of traditional knowledge.

Defender-Wilson has been widely recognized for her accomplishments, serving as a board member for Arts Midwest, the North Dakota Council on the Arts, and the North Dakota Centennial Commission. For her, though, the reward is not the public recognition but knowing the value of her stories and teaching them to others. "The entire life I've come through so far with our stories has helped me relate to, communicate with, and respect other people because I relate to, communicate with, and respect my own culture." The power of stories, she said, illustrates that "history is always there- - you're standing there dragging all these things behind you."

White Buffalo (Cheyenne, born in 1862) died in June 1929. He was described in newspaper articles in 1902 as being of striking appearance, as his hair had turned completely white when he was very young. His photo from his Carlisle days, dressed in a suit with a short haircut in the white man's style, shows that to be true. In 1888, when he was 26, he married a full-blood Northern Cheyenne widow. Medicine Woman, who was 30 at the time. She had also been born in Montana as had her parents. On the 1905 Indian Census for their reservation, they had four children listed: Emma White Buffalo, son Receiving Roots, Paul White Buffalo and Pratt White Buffalo - named for the Carlisle School founder. On the 1910 U. S. Federal Census, they are listed with only three of seven surviving children: John White Buffalo, James White Buffalo and Fred White Buffalo. According to the 1910 census, the mother of Medicine Woman also lived with them as well, 76 at the time, widowed and named Siege Woman. Medicine Woman is listed on this census as illiterate, as is her mother. His son, John White Buffalo enlisted for service in World War I. As full blood Cheyenne, both White Buffalo and Medicine Woman received land allotments on the reservation in 1891 in Lincoln Township in present-day Blaine County, Oklahoma. These are listed on several of the Indian Census lists as allotments number 966 and 967. White Buffalo lived to be 67 years old, and passed away on June 23, 1929, per the 1930 Indian census for the reservation. According to his obituary in the Watonga Republican newspaper dated June 27, 1929, he is buried at the Indian Mission Church on the reservation and was survived by his wife and sons.

American Horse was a Shrewd Sioux Chief and one of the wittiest and shrewdest of the Sioux chiefs, who succeeded to the name and position of an uncle, killed in the battle of Slim Buttes in 1876. The younger American Horse was born a little before the encroachments of the whites upon the Sioux country became serious and their methods aggressive, and his early manhood brought him into that most trying and critical period of our history. He had been tutored by his uncle since his own father was killed in battle while he was still very young. The American Horse band was closely attached to a trading post, and its members, in consequence, were inclined to be friendly with the whites, a policy closely adhered to by their leader.

When he was born, his old grandfather said: "Put him out in the sun! Let him ask his great-grandfather, the Sun, for the warm blood of a warrior!" And he had warm blood. He was a genial man, liking notoriety and excitement. He always seized an opportunity to leap into the center of the arena.

In early life, he was a clownish sort of boy among the boys —an expert mimic and impersonator. This talent made him popular and in his way a leader. He was a natural actor, and early showed marked ability as a speaker.

American Horse was about ten years old when he was attacked by three Crow warriors while driving a herd of ponies to water. Here he displayed native cunning and initiative. It seemed he had scarcely a chance to escape, for the enemy was near. He yelled frantically at the ponies to start them toward home, while he dropped off into a thicket of willows and hid there.

A part of the herd was caught in sight of the camp and there was a counter chase, but the Crows got away with the ponies. Of course, his mother was frantic, believing her boy had been killed or captured; but after the excitement was over, he appeared in camp unhurt. When questioned about his escape, he remarked: "I knew they would not take the time to hunt for small game when there was so much bigger close by."

Moving Robe Woman, a Hunkpapa (Sitting Bull's branch of the Sioux). She was no stranger to battle. At age 17, she took part in a war party against the Crow. In July 1876, now at about age 23, she was among the Sioux and Lakota who camped at the Greasy Grass (Little Big Horn). On this fateful day, she was digging turnips when a warrior rode by warning women to take their children to the hills. General Custer was about to attack. Moving Robe Woman raced back to her lodge where she learned that her brother, One Hawk, was killed in an earlier battle with Custer's men. Now, in deep mourning and fueled by revenge, Moving Robe braided her hair, painted her face red, mounted her horse, and with her brother's war staff in hand, galloped into battle. "I was a woman," she reportedly said, "But I was not afraid." Her determination emboldened the male warriors to fight ferociously for their way of life, in what would end up an overwhelming victory for the Native Americans. Custer's entire cavalry, 268 men, himself included, were killed—at least one at the hands of Moving Robe. She may have gotten her vengeance, but it was bitter, and it came at a cost. She later said, "No one staged a victory dance that night. They were mourning their own dead." Moving Robe Woman died in 1935 at Standing Rock Reservation in South Dakota. She was about 81 years old.

The Shoshone are an Indigenous tribe, who originated in the western Great Basin and spread north and east into present-day Idaho and Wyoming. By 1500, some Eastern Shoshone had crossed the Rocky Mountains into the Great Plains. Shoshone, 1880.

A little Pikuni (Blackfeet) Boy - Children are sacred in all Indigenous cultures. Protect our children and keep them with their families. Children wore small versions of adult clothing, included beaded outfits and dresses, along with ceremonial items such as headdresses. Boys usually wore nothing but breechcloths during warm weather, as did many men. The ears of children were pierced quite early, usually by older women who first recounted four noted deeds — like warriors — regarding such work as hide tanning and lodge (tipi) making. The main time to pierce ears was during Sun Dance inside the Medicine Lodge. Pikuni children learned by watching their elders and imitating their actions.

Medicine Crow, was born around 1848 in the area of the Musselshell, member of the New Made Lodge Acirarī'o clan and of the Lumpwood warrior society. According to his grandson, tribal historian and storyteller Joe Medicine Crow, Medicine Crow's father, a prominent headman, was called Jointed Together and his mother was One Buffalo Calf. He wasn't yet born when his father died, probably in the smallpox epidemic; his mother later married the noted medicine man Look At The Bulls Penis (better known as Sees The Living Bull or Bull Goes Hunting), who became an important figure in Medicine Crow's youth. It is said that he looked for a vision at least three times; the fourth time, when he was eighteen, he fasted for 4 days and 3 nights; the fourth night, he had the vision of a white man who told him that he came from the land of the rising sun, and that many others like were coming to the Crow land and take possession of it. He then advised Medicine Crow of not opposing the newcomers, the White Eyes, and exhorted him to "deal with them wisely, and all would have turned out all right". It is said that in other visions Medicine Crow foresaw the passing away of the buffalo, the building of the Big Horn Southern Railroad ("something black with round legs puffing smoke and pulling boxlike objects behind it") and of planes ("wagons flying in the sky"). His medicine were the hawk and the eagle (even if, according to some reports, he had to "borrow" them, as he didn't manage to get them in a personal vision).

He joined his first war party at 15 and, for the following nineteen years, he got the honors required to obtain chieftainship. He is said to have counted

3 first coups, wrestled away 5 weapons from an enemy, stolen 2 horses cutting the halter rope, and commanded 10 successful war parties. In tribal warfare, he made his most famous exploits against the Lakotas (sometimes together with his friend, River Crow Two Leggings): in 1874, he and his party annihilated 7 Lakotas entrenched in a deep washout; the Lakotas had already killed several Crows when Medicine Crow jumped with his horse in the washout, panicking the enemies who fled and were quickly dispatched.

In 1876 Medicine Crow, together with other 176 Crows, joined general George Crook's troops and fought in the Battle of the Rosebud (according to Joe Medicine Crow, it was Medicine Crow to "carry the pipe" for the Crow scouts, while Plenty Coups told Frank Linderman that he himself led the Crow warriors – Alligator Stands Up). Lt. John Bourke thus remembered the Crow leader "…Medicine Crow, the Crow chief, looked like a devil in his war bonnet of feathers, furs and buffalo horns".

In 1877 Medicine Crow joined again the US troops in the fights against the Nez Percés. During a battle, a Nez Percé challenged him to combat and shot Medicine Crow's horse under him. Medicine Crow went on his charge, jumping from side to side until he pounced on the Nez Percé, wrestling his weapon away from him and then allowing him to rejoin his comrades (Crow used to be allies of the Nez Percés).

In 1880 Medicine Crow, together with a delegation composed of other five tribesmen went to Washington, D.C. to discuss settlements in the Crow agency, the selling of Crow lands and the eventual division of the land into individual farms. Medicine Crow later settled in Lodge Grass Creek, taking up farming and playing an important role during the 1887 Sword Bearer incident when, together with Pretty Eagle and Plenty Coups, he managed to keep the tribe united. During the early 1900s, he opposed firmly the selling of the Crow lands and in 1890 he was appointed as tribal judge.

Medicine Crow died in 1920 and is buried on the Valley of Chieftains (in the Little Big Horn area). He is said to have taken 6 wives; from the last one, Medicine Sheep, he had 4 sons (Cassie, Hugh, Leo and Chester). **Leo Medicine Crow** fathered Chief Joseph Medicine Crow, who's now 96 and considered one of the official tribal historians.

On February 22, 1876, **Thaté Iyóhiwiŋ** was a Yankton Dakota woman living on the Yankton Indiana Reservation in South Dakota, and her European American mate, Felker Simmons, brought their daughter,

Zitkála-Šá, into the world. Simmons would abandon mother and child, yet Zitkála-Šá describes the first 8 years of her life on the reservation as happy and safe. All that changed in 1884 when missionaries came to "save" the children.

Even though White's Indiana Manual Labor Institute was a Quaker project, it still forced the children who attended to adapt to the Quaker way of doing things, including taking new names. Zitkála-Šá was renamed Gertrude Simmons. In her biographies, Zitkála-Šá describes deep conflict between her native identity and the dominant white culture, the sorrow of being separated from her mother, and her joy in learning to read, write, and play the violin.

Zitkála-Šá returned to the reservation in 1887, but after 3 years she decided she wanted to further her education and returned to the Institute again. She taught music while attending school from 1891 to 1895, when she earned her first diploma. Her speech at graduation tackled the issue of women's inequality and was praised in local newspapers. She had a gift of public speaking and music, and put both to good use during her life.

In 1895 Zitkála-Šá earned a scholarship to attend Earlham College in Richmond, Indiana. While in college she gave public speeches and even translated Native American legends into Latin and English for children. In 1887, mere weeks from graduation, her health took a turn for the worse; her scholarship did not cover all expenses, so she had to drop out.

After college Zitkála-Šá used her musical talents to make a living. From 1897-1899, she played violin with the New England Conservatory of Music in Boston. She then took a job teaching music at the Carlisle Indian Industrial School in Pennsylvania, where she also hosted debates on the issue of Native American treatment. The school used her to recruit students and impress the world, but her speaking out against their rigid indoctrination ofnative children into white culture resulted in her dismissal in 1901. Concerned about her mother's health, Zitkála-Šá returned to the reservation. While there she began to collect the stories of her people and translate them into English. She found a publisher in Ginn and Company, and they put out her collection of these stories as Old Indian Legends in 1901. Like most authors, she took another job at the Bureau of Indian Affairs as her principal support. It was at this job in 1902 that she met and married Captain Raymond Bonnin, a mixed-race Nakota man.

The couple moved to work on the Uintah-Ouray Reservation in Utah for the next 14 years. They had one son, named Ohiya. Zitkála-Šá met and began to collaborate with William F. Hanson, a composer at Brigham Young University. Together they created The Sun Dance, the first opera co-written by a Native American. The opera used the backdrop of the Ute Sun Dance to explore Ute and Yankton Dakota cultures. It premiered in 1913 and was originally performed by Ute actors and singers. Choosing such a topic for the opera would have been a way to strike back at forced enculturation, because the ritual itself had been outlawed by the Federal Government in 1883 and remained so until 1933. Much later, in 1938, The Sun Dance came to The Broadway Theatre in New York City.

From 1902-1916, Zitkála-Šá published several articles about her life and native legends for English readers. Her works appeared in Atlantic Monthly and Harper's Monthly, magazines with primarily a white readership. Her essays also appeared in American Indian Magazine. While these pieces were often autobiographical, they were still political and social commentary that showed her increased frustration with the Bureau of Indian Affairs, which fired the couple in 1916.

In 1916, the couple moved to Washington D.C., where Zitkála-Šá served as the secretary of the Society of the American Indian. In 1926, she founded the National Council of American Indians, an organization that worked to improve the treatment and lives of Native Americans. By 1928, she was an advisor to the Meriam Commission, which would lead to several improvements in how the Federal Government treated native peoples.

Zitkála-Šá continued writing, and her books and essays became more political in such works as American Indian Stories (1921) and "Oklahoma's Poor Rich Indians," published in 1923 by the Indian Rights Association. She spoke out for Indian's rights and women's rights up until her death in 1938 at the age of 61+. In the movies, male Native American warriors rode off to battle while their female counterparts remained behind to cook, sew, and take care of the camp. In real life, this wasn't always the case. Many warrior Native American women fought alongside men. The most famous of these was probably **Buffalo Calf Road Woman,** a member of the Northern Cheyenne tribe who fought in the Battle of the Rosebud and the Battle of Little Bighorn. In fact, according to the elders of the Northern Cheyenne tribe, it was she who dealt Custer his final deadly blow. Buffalo Calf Road Woman is just one of many incredible women you didn't read about in history class.

Fool Thunder and family (Hunkpapa Lakota) - The Hunkpapa (Lakota: Húŋkpapȟa) are a Native American group, one of the seven council fires of the Lakota tribe. The name Húŋkpapȟa is a Lakota word, meaning "Head of the Circle" (at one time, the tribe's name was represented in EuropeanAmerican records as Honkpapa). By tradition, the Húŋkpapȟa set up their lodges at the entryway to the circle of the Great Council when the Sioux met in convocation. They speak Lakȟóta, one of the three dialects of the Sioux language.

Seven hundred and fifty mounted Yankton, Yanktonai and Lakota joined six companies of the Sixth Infantry and 80 fur trappers in an attack on an Arikara Indian village at Grand River (now South Dakota) in August 1823, named the Arikara War. Members of the Lakota, a part of them "Ankpapat", were the first Native Americans to fight in the American Indian Wars alongside US forces west of the Missouri.

They may have formed as a tribe within the Lakota relatively recently, as the first mention of the Hunkpapa in European-American historical records was from a treaty of 1825.

By signing the 1825 treaty, the Hunkpapa and the United States committed themselves to keep up the "friendship which has heretofore existed". With their x-mark, the chiefs also recognized the supremacy of the United States. It is not certain whether they really understood the text in the document. The US representatives gave a medal to Little White Bear, who they understood was the principal Hunkpapa chief; they did not realize how decentralized Native American authority was.

With the Indian Vaccination Act of 1832, the United States assumed responsibility for the inoculation of the Indians against smallpox. Some visiting Hunkpapa may have benefitted from Dr. M. Martin's vaccination of about 900 southern Lakota (no divisions named) at the head of Medicine Creek that autumn. When smallpox struck in 1837, it hit the Hunkpapa as the northernmost Lakota division. The loss, however, may have been fewer than one hundred people. Overall, the Hunkpapa seem to have suffered less from new diseases than many other tribes did.

The boundaries for the Lakota Indian territory were defined in the general peace treaty negotiated near Fort Laramie in the summer of 1851. Leaders of eight different tribes, often at odds with each other and each claiming large territories, signed the treaty. The United States was a ninth party to it. The Crow Indian territory included a tract of land north of the

Yellowstone, while the Little Bighorn River ran through the heartland of the Crow country (now Montana). The treaty defines the land of the Arikara, the Hidatsa and the Mandan as a mutual area north of Heart River, partly encircled by the Missouri (now North Dakota).

Soon enough the Hunkpapa and other Sioux attacked the Arikara and the two other so-called village tribes, just as they had done in the past. By 1854, these three smallpox-devastated tribes called for protection from the U.S. Army, and they would repeatedly do so almost to the end of inter-tribal warfare. Eventually the Hunkpapa and other Lakota took control of the three tribes' area north of Heart River, forcing the village people to live in Like a Fishhook Village outside their treaty land. The Lakota were largely in control of the occupied area to 1876–1877.

The United States Army General Warren estimated the population of the Hunkpapa Lakota at about 2920 in 1855. He described their territory as ranging "from the Big Cheyenne up to the Yellowstone, and west to the Black Hills. He states that they formerly intermarried extensively with the Cheyenne." He noted that they raided settlers along the Platte River In addition to dealing with warfare, they suffered considerable losses due to contact with Europeans and contracting of Eurasian infectious diseases to which they had no immunity.

The Hunkpapa gave some of their remote relatives among the Santee Sioux armed support during a large-scale battle near Killdeer Mountain in 1864 with U.S. troops led by General A. Sully.

The Great Sioux Reservation was established with a new treaty in 1868. The Lakota agreed to the construction of "any railroad" outside their reservation. The United States recognized that "the country north of the North Platte River and east of the summits of the Big Horn Mountains" was unsold or unceded Indian territory. These hunting grounds in the south and in the west of the new Lakota domain were used mainly by the Sicangu (Brule-Sioux) and the Oglala, living nearby.

The "free bands" of Hunkpapa favored campsites outside the unsold areas. They took a leading part in the westward enlargement of the range used by the Lakota in the late 1860s and the early 1870s at the expense of other tribes. In search for buffalo, Lakota regularly occupied the eastern part of the Crow Indian Reservation as far west as the Bighorn River, sometimes even raiding the Crow Agency, as they did in 1873. The Lakota pressed the

Crow Indians to the point that they reacted like other small tribes: they called for the U.S. Army to intervene and take actions against the intruders.

In the late summer of 1873, the Hunkpapa boldly attacked the Seventh Cavalry in United States territory north of the Yellowstone. Custer's troops escorted a railroad surveying party here, due to similar attacks the year before. Battles such as Honsinger Bluff and Pease Bottom took place on land purchased by the United States from the Crow tribe on May 7, 1868. These continual attacks, and complaints from American Natives, prompted the Commissioner of Indian Affairs to assess the full situation on the northern plains. He said that the unfriendly Lakota roaming the land of other people should "be forced by the military to come in to the Great Sioux Reservation". That was in 1873, notably one year before the discovery of gold in the Black Hills, but the US government did not take action on this concept until three years later.

The Hunkpapa were among the victors in the Battle of Little Bighorn in the Crow Indian Reservation in July 1876.

Since the 1880s, most Hunkpapa have lived in the Standing Rock Indian Reservation (in North and South Dakota). It comprises land along the Grand River which had been used by the Arikara Indians in 1823; the Hunkpapa "won the west" half a century before the whites.

During the 1870s, when the Native Americans of the Great Plains were fighting the United States, the Hunkpapa were led by Sitting Bull in the fighting, together with the Oglala Lakota. They were among the last of the tribes to go to the reservations. By 1891, the majority of Hunkpapa Lakota, about 571 people, resided in the Standing Rock Indian Reservation of North and South Dakota. Since then they have not been counted separately from the rest of the Lakota.

Comanche Little Chief (self-name NERMERNUH) - Native American Tribe of Equstrian nomads whose 18th & 19th Century territory comprised the Southern Great Plains. The name Comanche is deprived from a Ute word, meaning "anyone who wants to fight all the time", the Comanche had previously been part of the Wyoming Shoshone Tribe.

The Cheyenne Indians are from the Great Plains. Many people don't know this but the Cheyenne consists of two tribes. One tribe is called Sotaeo'o and the other is the Tsitsistas. The name Cheyenne means "Little Cree". Many Cheyenne lived in Montana and Oklahoma. Early Cheyenne lived in earth lodges and ate mostly fish to survive. It was in the early 1800's that the Cheyenne moved into teepees and started hunting wild animals for their meals. The Cheyenne Indians then spread out, living not only in Montana and Oklahoma, but could be found in Colorado, South Dakota, and Wyoming.

The 19th century brought on the Indian Wars. While the Cheyenne Indians were friendly with any settlers they met, the Colorado Militia and Lt Custer's Calvary attacked and killed many peaceful Indians. After this, the Cheyenne Indian became hostile and was considered the enemy of any settlers. It is believed that the Cheyenne Indians along with the Lakota and Arapaho tribes gathered together near the Little Bighorn River in the late 1800's forming the largest gathering of Indians that numbered more than 10,000.

When this news reached Washington, this angered the Army and they sought to capture the Cheyenne. When northern Indians were captured, they were moved to the south, which caused the Indians to become ill. Many caught malaria in their new home and asked to return to their northern home. More than one million Cheyenne Indians traveled back north but the Army and many volunteers were pursuing the Indians in hopes of ridding their tribe forever.

As the Indian group split into two groups, one made it home but the other was captured and held in Nebraska. They were held without water, food or heating and soon decided to revolt. When the Cheyenne Indians decided to escape they were gunned down by the Army. Sadly, it was thought that only about 50 Cheyenne Indians survived. Today the Cheyenne Indian have grown to over 20,000 and has continued to retain their unique language and lifestyle.

Rain-in-the-Face was a leader of the Lakota tribe. He was among those who defeated George Armstrong Custer and the US 7th Cavalry Regiment at the 1876 Battle of Little Big Horn.

Born in the Dakota Territory near the forks of the Cheyenne River in about 1835, Rain-in-the-Face was from the Hunkpapa band of the Lakota nation. His name may have been given to him due to a fight with a Cheyenne boy when he was pretty young. His face was splattered like rain with his Cheyenne adversary's blood.

Late in his life, he related that the name was reinforced by an incident when he was a young man in a battle in a heavy rainstorm with a band of Gros

Ventres. At the end of the lengthy combat, his face was streaked with war paint.

He first fought against the whites in 1866 in a raid against Fort Totten in what is now North Dakota. He again fought the U.S. Army in the Fetterman massacre near Fort Phil Kearny in present-day Montana in the same year. In the Black Hills War, he led a raid at the Tongue River in which two white civilians accompanying Custer's cavalry were killed. He returned to the Standing Rock Reservation but was captured by Custer after being betrayed by reservation Indians. He was taken to Fort Abraham Lincoln and incarcerated. However, he was freed by a sympathetic soldier and returned to the reservation, then fled to the Powder River. In the spring of 1876, he joined the hostile Sioux under Sitting Bull and traveled with him to the Little Big Horn River in early June.

During the subsequent fighting on Custer Hill on June 26, Rain-in-the-Face is alleged to have cut the heart out of Thomas Custer, a feat that was popularized by American poet Henry Wadsworth Longfellow in "The Revenge of Rain in the Face." According to legend, Tom Custer had unjustly imprisoned Rain-in-the-Face. Some contemporary accounts claimed that the Rain-in-the-Face had personally dispatched George Custer as well, but in the confused fighting, a number of similar claims have been attributed to other warriors.

Rain-in-the-Face died at his home in Bullhead Station on the Standing Rock Reservation in North Dakota after a lengthy illness.

Member of the Dreaded Cheyenne Dog Soldiers - It is written in some texts that they participated in Battle of the Greasy Grass (Little Big Horn). They did not. The Cheyenne contingent at Greasy Grass were Northern Cheyenne; a different tribe, with their own dialect and religious practices. Dog Soldiers (Southern Cheyenne), also referred to as 'Dog leash men' (they wore a leash, similar to the Lakota 'sash wearers') took responsibility for the tribe's security, both internal and external. Selected for bravery, discipline and fighting skills, they maintained order in the camp.

If a hunt was planned, they would see to it that pairs of young warriors, did not sneak off to go out and get the first kill for example. Similarly, when instructions were given to break camp, they would do a full perimeter inspection and literally whip stragglers to pack up with the other people. In battles, designated Dogmen were appointed to pin themselves to the ground (via leash and cattle pin) and fight to the death if necessary, allowing the main body to withdraw from the scene unhindered. They could not leave that dead ground under their feet, unless relieved by another Dog Soldier, or their party had departed completely.

A Blackfoot Legend – The Story of the Buffalo Dance

When the buffalo first came to be upon the land, they were not friendly to the people.

When the hunters tried to coax them over the cliffs for the good of the villages, they were reluctant to offer themselves up.

They did not relish being turned into blankets and dried flesh for winter rations.

They did not want their hooves and horn to become tools and utensils nor did they welcome their sinew being used for sewing.

"No, no," they said.

"We won't fall into your traps.

And we will not fall for your tricks."

So when the hunters guided them towards the abyss, they would always turn aside at the very last moment. With this lack of cooperation, it seemed the villagers would be hungry and cold and ragged all winter long.

One of the hunters had a daughter who was very proud of the father's skill with the bow. During the fullness of summer, he always brought her the best of hides to dress, and she in turn would work the deerskins into the softest, whitest of garments for him to wear. Her own dresses were like the down of a snow goose, and the moccasins she made for the children and the grandmothers in the village were the most welcome gifts.

But now with the hint of snow on the wind, and deer becoming more scarce in the willow breaks, she could see this reluctance on the part of the buffalo families could become a real problem.

Hunter's Daughter decided she would do something about it.

She went to the base of the cliff and looked up. She began to sing in a low, soft voice, "Oh, buffalo family, come down and visit me. If you come down and feed my relatives in a wedding feast, I will join your family as the bride of your strongest warrior."

As she stopped and listened, she thought she heard the slight rumbling sound of thunder in the distance.

Again she sang, "Oh, buffalo family, come down and visit me. Feed my family in a wedding feast so that I may be a bride."

The thunder was much louder now. Suddenly the buffalo family began falling from the sky at her feet. One very large bull landed on top of the others, and walked across the backs of his relatives to stand before the hunter's daughter.

"I am here to claim you as my bride," said Large Buffalo.

"Oh, but now I am afraid to go with you," said Hunter's Daughter.

"Ah, but you must," said Large Buffalo, "For my people have come to provide your people with a wedding feast. As you can see, they have offered themselves up."

"Yes, but I must run and tell my relatives the good news," said Hunter's Daughter.

"No," said Large Buffalo. "No word need be sent. You are not getting away so easily."
And with that said, Large Buffalo lifted her between his horns and carried her off to his village in the rolling grass hills.

The next morning the whole village was out looking for Hunter's Daughter. When they found the mound of buffalo below the cliff, the father, who was in fact a fine tracker as well as a skilled hunter, looked at his daughter's footprints in the dust.

"Shes' gone off with a buffalo," he said. "I shall follow them and bring her back."

So Hunter walked out upon the plains, with only his bow and arrows as companions. He walked and walked a great distance until he was so tires that he had to sit down to rest beside a buffalo wallow.

Along came Magpie and sat down beside him.

Hunter spoke to Magpie in a respectful tone. "O knowledgeable bird, has my daughter been stolen from me by a buffalo? Have you seen them? Can you tell me where they have gone?"

Magpie replied with understanding, "Yes, I have seen them pass this way. They are resting just over this hill."

"Well," said Hunter, "would you kindly take my daughter a message for me? Will you tell her I am here just over the hill?"

So Magpie flew to where Large Buffalo lay asleep amidst his relatives in the dry prairie grass. He hopped over to where Hunter's Daughter was "quilling" moccasins, as she sat dutifully beside her sleeping husband. "Your father is waiting for you on the other side of the hill," whispered Magpie to the Maiden.

"Oh, this is very dangerous," she told him. "These buffalo are not friendly to us and they might try to hurt my father if he should come this way. Please tell him to wait for me and I will try to slip away to see him."

Just then her husband, Large Buffalo, awoke and took off his horn. "Go bring me a drink from the wallow just over this hill," said her husband.

So she took the horn in her hand and walked very casually over the hill.

Her father motioned silently for her to come with him, as he bent into a low crouch in the grass. "No," she whispered. "The buffalo are angry with our people who have killed their people. They will run after us and trample us into the dirt. I will go back and see what I can do to soothe their feelings."

And so Hunter's Daughter took the horn of water back to her husband who gave a loud snort when he took a drink. The snort turned into a bellow and all of the buffalo got up in alarm. They all put their tails in the air and danced a buffalo dance over the hill, trampling the hunter to pieces.

His daughter sat down on the edge of the wallow and broke into tears.

"Why are you crying?" said her buffalo husband.

"You have killed my father and I am a prisoner, besides," she sobbed.

"Well, what of my people?" her husband replied. "We have given our children, our parents and some of our wives up to your relatives in exchange for your presence among us. A deal is a deal."

But after some consideration of her feelings, Large Buffalo knelt down beside her and said to her, "If you can bring your father back to life again, we will let him take you back home to your people."

So Hunter's Daughter started to sing a little song. "Magpie, Magpie help me find some piece of my father which I can mend back whole again."

Magpie appeared and sat down in front of her with his head cocked to the side.

"Magpie, Magpie, please see what you can find," she sang softly to the wind which bent the grasses slightly apart. Magpie cocked his head to the side and looked carefully within the layered folds of the grasses as the wind sighed again.

Quickly he picked out a piece of her father that had been hidden there, a little bit of bone.

"That will be enough to do the trick," said Hunter's Daughter, as she put the bone on the ground and covered it with her blanket. And then she started to sing a reviving song that had the power to bring injured people back to the land of the living. Quietly she sang the song that her grandmother had taught her. After a few melodious passages, there was a lump under the blanket.

She and Magpie looked under the blanket and could see a man, but the man was not breathing. He lay cold as stone. So Hunter's Daughter continued to sing, a little softer, and a little softer, so as not to startle her father as he began to move. When he stood up, alive and strong, the buffalo people were amazed.

They said to Hunter's Daughter, "Will you sing this song for us after every hunt? We will teach your people the buffalo dance, so that whenever you dance before the hunt, you will be assured a good result. Then you will sing this song for us, and we will all come back to live again."

Bill Pickett (ca 1870-1932) - African American Cowboy inventor of "bulldogging," a rodeo technique to wrestle a steer to the ground.

From 1905 to 1931, the Miller brothers' 101 Ranch Wild West Show was one of the great shows in the tradition begun by William F. "Buffalo Bill" Cody in 1883. The 101 Ranch Show introduced bulldogging (steer wrestling), an exciting rodeo event invented by Bill Pickett, one of the show's stars.

Riding his horse, Spradley, Pickett came alongside a Longhorn steer, dropped to the steer's head, twisted its head toward the sky, and bit its upper lip to get full control. Cowdogs of the Bulldog breed were known to bite the lips of cattle to subdue them. That's how Pickett's technique got the name "bulldogging." As the event became more popular among rodeo cowboys, the lip biting became increasingly less popular until it disappeared from steer wrestling altogether. Bill Pickett, however, became an immortal rodeo cowboy, and his fame has grown since his death.

He died in 1932 as a result of injuries received from working horses at the 101 Ranch. His grave is on what is left of the 101 Ranch property near Ponca City, Oklahoma. Pickett was inducted into the National Rodeo Hall of Fame in 1972 for his contribution to the sport.

Bill Pickett was the second of thirteen children born to Thomas Jefferson and Mary Virginia Elizabeth (Gilbert) Pickett, both of whom were former slaves. He began his career as a cowboy after completing the fifth grade. Bill soon began giving exhibitions of his roping, riding and bulldogging skills, passing a hat for donations.

By 1888, his family had moved to Taylor, Texas, and Bill performed in the town's first fair that year. He and his brothers started a horse-breaking business in Taylor, and Bill was a member of the national guard and a deacon of the Baptist church. In December 1890, Bill married Maggie Turner.

Known by the nicknames "The Dusky Demon" and "The Bull-Dogger," Pickett gave exhibitions in Texas and throughout the West. His performance in 1904 at the Cheyenne Frontier Days (America's best-known rodeo) was considered extraordinary and spectacular. He signed on with the 101 Ranch show in 1905, becoming a full-time ranch employee in 1907. The next year, he moved his wife and children to Oklahoma.

He later performed in the U.S., Canada, Mexico, South America, and England, and became the first black cowboy movie star. Had he not been banned from competing with white rodeo contestants, Pickett might have become one of the greatest record-setters in his sport. He was often identified as an Indian, or some other ethnic background other than black, to be allowed to compete. Bill Pickett died April 2, 1932, after being kicked in the head by a horse. Famed humorist Will Rogers announced the funeral of his friend on his radio show. In 1989, years after being honored by the National Rodeo Hall of Fame, Pickett was inducted into the Prorodeo Hall of Fame and Museum of the American Cowboy at Colorado Springs, Colorado. A 1994 U.S. postage stamp meant to honor Pickett accidentally showed one of his brothers.

Cochise (1874, Arizona) - Cochise led the Chiricahua Apache tribe during a period of violent social upheaval. In 1850, the United States took control of what is today Arizona and New Mexico. At first, he showed no hostility to the white settlers and kept the peace. Cochise is reputed to be a strategist and leader who has never been defeated in battle. For 10 years, Cochise and his warriors fought the white settlers. Cochise surrendered to American forces in 1871. After his death, he was secretly buried somewhere in or near his impregnable fortress in the Dragoon Mountains. His descendants live on the Mescalero Apache.

As Comanche (Nummuhnuh) power began to tower over the Southern Great Plains, a rich harvest of horses awaited them in northern Mexico. Comanche warriors rounded up thousands of horses, cattle, mules, and many captives. In the early to the mid-1800's, the war parties struck like lightning successfully raiding ranches and haciendas. Comanche warriors went anywhere they wanted to go and did anything they wanted to do. They struck south to Durango which was within five hundred miles of Mexico City. Comanche war parties also boldly swept over Chihuahua, Zacatecas, Tamaulipas, Coahuila, Nuevo Leon, and San Luis. On the northern frontier of Mexico, a great many ranches were simply overwhelmed by the Comanches.

Comanche Chief Quanah Parker - The leader of the raid always travels first. After looking at the others in the camp, a council is then convened. He then excitedly shares:

"Back in the village, I decided to go to war - everybody knows it, women and children - Now I see you here, I feel glad, a big party - we are going to war."

Impressive picture of famed Comanche Chief Quanah Parker with bow and arrows, circa 1891. Photograph courtesy of the Bureau of American Ethnology, Oklahoma Native American Photographs Collection, Gilcrease Museum, Tulsa, Oklahoma.

The Cheyenne Warrior, Red Blanket - He held a tomahawk. Some warriors favored the tomahawk, others the battle axe, and for some the war club; used to 'brain' the enemy. Apaches preferred the war club, it was hit and go, while a tomahawk could stall the mounted/dismounted warrior; getting embedded in the enemy, and would have to be pried loose occasionally.

Mildred Imoch Glaghorn was a traditional doll maker, schoolteacher, and Fort Sill Apache tribal leader, Mildred Imoch (En-Ohn or Lay-a-Bet) was born a prisoner of war at Fort Sill, Oklahoma, on December 11, 1910. Her grandfather had followed Geronimo into battle, and her grandparents and parents were imprisoned with the Chiricahua Apache in Florida, Alabama, and at Fort Sill. Her family was one of only seventy-five that chose to remain at Fort Sill instead of relocating to the Mescalero Reservation in New Mexico in 1913.

Mildred Cleghorn attended school in Apache, Oklahoma, at Haskell Institute in Kansas, and at Oklahoma State University, receiving a degree in home economics in 1941. After she finished her formal education, she spent several years as a home extension agent in Kansas, Oklahoma, and New Mexico, and then worked for sixteen years as a home economics teacher, first at Fort Sill Indian School at Lawton and then at Riverside Indian School at Anadarko. Later, she taught kindergarten at Apache Public School in Apache. She was married to William G. Cleghorn, whom she had met in Kansas, and their union produced a daughter, Peggy. In 1976 Mildred Cleghorn became chairperson of the Fort Sill Apache Tribe, newly organized as a self-governing entity. Her leadership in that government revolved around preserving traditional history and culture. She retired from the post at age eighty-five in 1995.

Cleghorn's many awards and recognitions included a human relations fellowship at Fisk University in 1955, the Ellis Island Award in 1987, and the Indian of the Year Award in 1989. She also served as an officer in the North American Indian Women's Association, as secretary of the Southwest Oklahoma Intertribal Association, and as treasurer of the American Indian Council of the Reformed Church of America. Above all, Mildred Cleghorn was a cultural leader. She spent a lifetime creating dolls authentically clothed to represent forty of the tribes she had encountered in her teaching career. Her work was exhibited at the Smithsonian Institution in Washington, D.C. Her life ended in an automobile accident near Apache on April 15, 1997

The Miami people, are a Native American nation, originally speaking one of the Algonquian languages. Among the peoples known as the Great Lakes tribes, it occupied territory, that is now identified as Indiana, southwest Michigan, and western Ohio. By 1846, most of the Miami had been removed, to Indian Territory (now Oklahoma). The Miami Tribe of Oklahoma, is the only federally recognized tribe of Miami Indians, in the United States. The Miami Nation of Indiana, is an unrecognized tribe.

Lame White Man, or Ve'hoe'no˙ hnehé (**c**. **1837 or 1839–1876**), was a Cheyenne battle chief who fought at the Battle of the Little Big Horn, June 25, 1876, and was killed there. He was the only Cheyenne chief to die in the battle. He was also known as Bearded Man (to the Lakota) and Mad Hearted Wolf (Hahk o ni). He was the husband of Twin Woman and father to Red Hat and Crane Woman. His grandson John Stands In Timber, born after his death, became the tribal historian of the Northern Cheyenne, and wrote the book, Cheyenne Memories (1967), based on the oral history of his people.

Vé'ho'énòhnéhe Lame White Man was born into the Southern Cheyenne but moved north after the Sand Creek Massacre of 1864. He was also known as Mad Hearted Wolf (Hahk o ni), attesting to his bravery. He married Twin Woman and had children with her.

He became a chief of the Elk Horn Society with the Northern Cheyenne. He still kept ties with the Southern Cheyenne, serving as council chief. He was part of a delegation to Washington, DC in 1873.

It has been written that during the battle, Lame White Man wore a captured cavalry jacket, which was found tied to the cantle of a saddle. This account is disputed by his grandson, John Stands In Timber. He stated that he wore nothing during the battle but a blanket tied to his waist and moccasins. This information was told to him by his grandmother Twin Woman.

Lame White Man was shot and killed by U.S. soldiers on the west slope of Battle Ridge, where he had led a charge. Later a Miniconjou Lakota warrior (believed to be Little Crow) mistook him for an Army Indian scout and scalped him before realizing his mistake. Lame White Man was the only Cheyenne chief to die at the Battle of the Little Bighorn.

Yellow Wolf - Hermene MoxMox (1855 -1935) - Yellow Wolf left to history one of the few narratives of the final days of the Long March of Chief Joseph, describing the harsh days before the Nez Perces' surrender to General Nelson A. Miles. Born Hermene Moxmox, a nephew of Chief Joseph, Yellow Wolf was a warrior during the Nez Perces' Long March; he was only twenty-one years of age at that time. He had already earned a reputation among the Nez Perce as a hunter and sharpshooter. He was also an expert at training horses.

During the last battle of the Long March, between September 30 and October 5, 1877, Joseph and most of the survivors decided to surrender. A small band, including Yellow Wolf, escaped and took refuge with Sitting Bull's Hunkpapas in Canada. Yellow Wolf's recollections are contained in Lucullus McWhorter's book, Yellow Wolf (1940). Yellow Wolf died at Colville, Washington, in 1935, shortly after completing the Narrative for the book.

Makhpiya-Luta - Red Cloud - For most of his life, Red Cloud was fighting. At first, it was to defend his Oglala people against the Pawnee and Crow tribes, but by the time he reached his forties, Red Cloud was fighting the white man. His efforts led to the defeat of Fort Phil Kearny in Wyoming in 1867 and kept soldiers at bay (and in fear) for the rest of the winter. In the two years that followed, the government signed the Fort Laramie Treaty and gave the Native Americans land in Wyoming, Montana, and South Dakota. But soon after, the Black Hills were invaded, and Red Cloud and his people lost their land. Until his death in 1909, Red Cloud tried other ways to make peace and preserve the culture of his people, working with government officials and agents to reach a fair agreement. For most of his life, Red Cloud was fighting. At first, it was to defend his Oglala people against the Pawnee and Crow tribes, but by the time he reached his forties, Red Cloud was fighting the white man. His efforts led to the defeat of Fort Phil Kearny in Wyoming in 1867 and kept soldiers at bay (and in fear) for the rest of the winter. In the two years that followed, the government signed the Fort Laramie Treaty and gave the Native Americans land in Wyoming, Montana, and South Dakota. But soon after, the Black Hills were invaded, and Red Cloud and his people lost their land. Until his death in 1909, Red Cloud tried other ways to make peace and preserve the culture of his people, working with government officials and agents to reach a fair agreement.

Chief Sitting Bull was a Hunkpapa Lakota leader who played a significant role in the Battle of Little Bighorn. He was known for his exceptional leadership skills and his unwavering commitment to his people. He led by example, fighting alongside his warriors rather than sitting back and commanding from a distance. Sitting Bull earned the respect of his people, not by ordering them around, but by working alongside them. He demonstrated courage, wisdom, and patience, which his followers learned and emulated. Similarly, Tecumseh was a great Shawnee chief and warrior, known for his strong leadership skills and his remarkable oratory abilities. Tecumseh's leadership style was based on leading by example, as he was willing to sacrifice his life for his people. He rallied the various tribes of the American Midwest to fight for their land, which had been unjustly taken by colonizers. He was a fierce warrior on the battlefield, and his courage inspired his people to emulate his bravery. Crazy Horse was a Lakota warrior, who led his people to victory against the US army in what is known as the Fetterman Massacre. He was a humble yet fierce leader who led his people by example. He displayed unwavering courage and selflessness, which inspired his followers to fight alongside him against their oppressors. Crazy Horse's humility was evident even in the way he dressed, as he wore plain clothing and refused to wear the traditional headdress of a leader. True leaders lead with their hearts and have an unwavering commitment to their sacred values and the well-being of their communities. The examples set by Sitting Bull, Tecumseh and Crazy Horse demonstrate that leading with humility and leading by example is the foundation of true greatness. These leaders were willing to put themselves in harm's way, live modestly, and fight alongside their followers, inspiring them to emulate their courage, integrity and selflessness. By John Gonzalez

Picture Collection

1. Gertrude Three Finger
2. Larry Sellers
3. Chief Dan George
4. Navajo tribe member wearing a Nayenezgani
5. Inuit mother and child
6. Nez Perce Black Eagle Edward Curtis
7. Chief Black Hair and daughter
8. Three Apache Brothers photo A. Miller 1880's
9. Ute warrior Wilbur S. Nye Collection
10. Cynthia Ann Parker (Comanche: Narua)
11. Muscogee Actor Will (Sonny) Sampson
12. Blackfoot 1787 a Piegan Warrior
13. Arapaho tribe family members standing outside their teepee.
14. Chief John Smith (Chippewa)
15. Elsie Vance Crestview (Apache)
16. Chief Big Tree (Kiowa) 1850
17. Lakota Medicine Man Black Eagle 1932
18. Chief Long Wolf and Family (Sioux)
19. Flying Hawk (Crow)
20. Brenda Schad (Cherokee Model)
21. Mildred Imoch (En-Om En or Lay-a-Bet) Apache leader Fort Sill
22. The Choctaw
23. High Bear (Lakota) Oglala Indian
24. Chief American Horse & Chief Red Cloud (Sioux)
25. Chief Iron Hawk (Lakota) Oglala 1900
26. Chief Two Moon (Cheyenne)
27. The Omaha Dance (Sioux)
28. Chief Running Antelope
29. Astina Men (Gios Ventro 1872)
30. Mary Frances Thompson Fisher Te' Ata (Ckickasaw)
31. The Quechan Tribe (The Yuma)
32. Chief Red Fish (Lakota - Oglala)
33. Sarah Winnemvcca (Paiute)
34. Apache Indians
35. Bear Belly Arika Warrior (North Dakota) 1909
36. Hunkpapa group (Lakota)
37. Washoe Tribe (Lake Tahoe) 1866

38. Kaw-U-Tz a addon Nation Maiden
39. Chief Quanah Parker with bow and arrows (Comanche) 1891
40. Crow Warrior Montana 1743
41. Quanah Parker with his two wives Topay and Chonie
42. Kiowa Women
43. Jay Silverheels Harold Jay Smith (Canadian Indian Actor)
44. Nampeyo Hopi-Tewa famous potter
45. Isabelle Perico Enjady (Apache) Chiricahue
46. Quanah Parker and mother
47. Wanada Parker Page (Comanche) 1882-1970
48. Lakota Sioux Women in 1899 & Lakota Sioux Woman now
49. Red Blanket (Cheyenne Warrior)
50. Chief Sitting Bull (Tatanka Iyotake) (Lakota) Hunkpapa 1890
51. Makhpiya-uta aka Red Cloud 1909
52. Southern Cheyenne sisters (El Reno Oklahoma territory) 1895
53. Sitting Bull and Family (Sioux) 1880
54. Yuma tribe member playing the flute (Arizona) 1900
55. American Indian in Grief
56. Dust Maker – Pete Mitchell (Ponca) Northern Nebraska 1898
57. The Ute Pass Trail originates below the springs of Manitou, CO
58. Chief Crazy Horse
59. Ute warrior with companion dog
60. Honii-Osasvists (Wolf in the Middle) (Cheyenne) 1800
61. Will Pickett (1870-1932) African American Cowboy (Cherokee)
62. Chochise (Apache) Chiricahue 1874
63. Iron Thunder, Crow Eagle, Fool Thunder, Slow White Buffalo, all holding peace pipes, (Dakota) circa 1880's
64. Two Apache Women Brushing Against and Little Squint Eyes
65. Chief Buffalo Sundown (George Jackson)
66. White Buffalo (Cheyenne) was born in 1862
67. White Buffalo (Cheyenne)
68. Bird Wild Hog Warrior (Cheyemme)
69. Floyd Westerman--Red Crow
70. Human and Bison
71. Gor-osimp (Shoshone warrior) 1885
72. Chief Fast Thunder (Wakinyan Ohank'o) 1839-1914
73. Black Family in one house no windows
74. Black Elk (Holy Man of the Oglala (Lakota) 1863
75. Henry Oscar (One Bull) (Lakota warrior)
76. Nanye-Hi Cherokee Nancy Ward
77. Two Guns (Chief White Calf) (Blackfoot)

78. Flying Hawk historian, educator, philosopher (Lakota)
79. Geronimo Chief of the Apache
80. Geraldine Keams (Navajo) actress Flagstaff, Arizona
81. Rose Bompard (Bird)   (Crow)Chiricahua Woman   (Apache)
82. Navajo Dancer
83. Standing Bear   (Lakota)
84. Chief Blue Horse (Oglala   1872
85. Indian Warrior
86. Chief Iron Tail
87. Cheyenne Girl   1885
88. Woman Washington Yakama State tribe
89. Medicine Crow Sheridan Wyoming 1900 by Louis R. Bostwick
90. Chief Thunderhawk   Cetan Wakiyan
91. Hash-Nash-Shut (Wasco) Indian
92. Bull Chief   (Crow)
93. Young Man of the Piegan tribe   1900
94. Chief Brave Buffalo
95. Cetan Wakiyan, Chief Thunderhawk
96. American Indian Woman
97. Chief Joseph
98. Wounded Knee Warriors   1890
99. Yellow Wolf (Hermene MoxMox)   1855-1935
100. Stella Walking Antelope (daughter of Morris Walking antelope and Mary Agatha George
101. Bird Rattle (Piegan man)   1908 photo by Edward S. Curtis
102. Chief American Horse   (Sioux)
103. Moving Robe Woman (Sioux warrior)   Hunkpapa
104. A little Pikuni boy   (Blackfeet)
105. Thate Iyohiwin (Yankton) Dakota woman
106. Chief Medicine Crow   1848
107. Buffalo Calf Road Woman (Northern Cheyenne warrior)
108. Lenna Geronimo's daughter   1900
109. Indian Dancer
110. Two young Mesdalero Apache Men 1888
111. Comache Little chief
112. Chief Wolf Robe   (Cheyenne)
113. Suzanne and Samuel Gover with their children (Pawnee Nation)
114. Rain-in-the-Face was a leader of the Lakota tribe
115. Miami from Indiana, Michigan & Ohio 1846 Native American

Gertrude Three Finger, a Cheyenne tribe member, 1892

William E. Irwin was a photographer who worked across Arizona, New Mexico, and Oklahoma during the 19th and 20th centuries. He captured several photos of Southwestern Native Americans while he was in the area. Gertrude Three Finger is the young woman in this photo. She was a member of the Cheyenne tribe and is wearing a traditional outfit that is accessorized with elk teeth.

Irwin photographed Gertrude more than once, this photo was one that was printed using an albumen print. You can see it in real life at the University of Oklahoma's library.

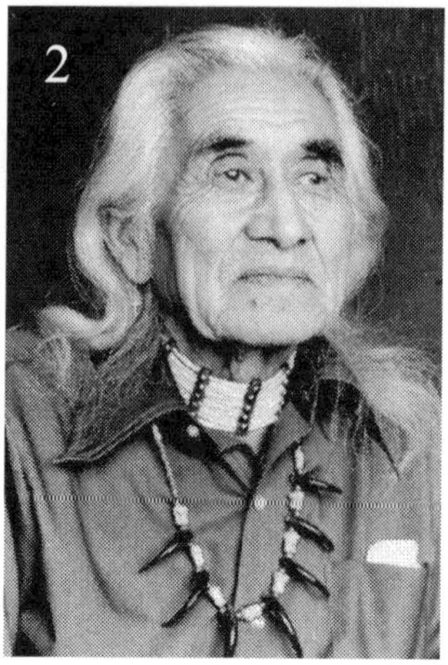
2

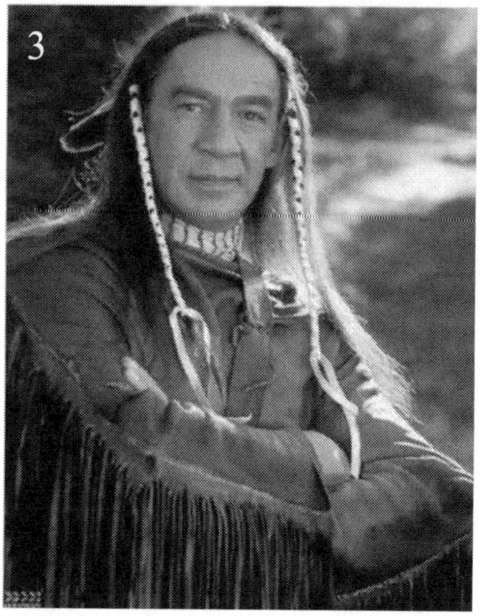
3

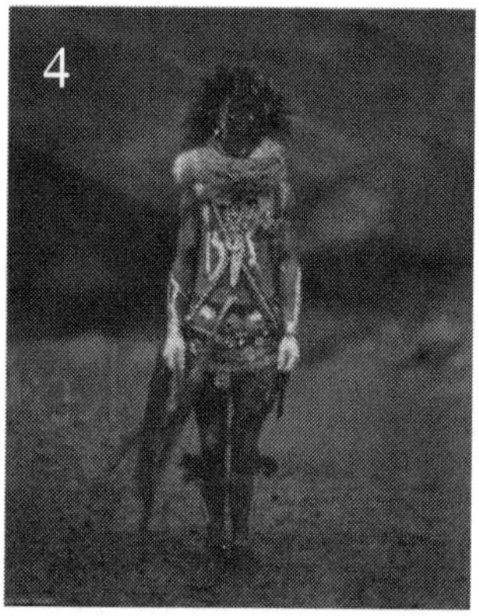
4

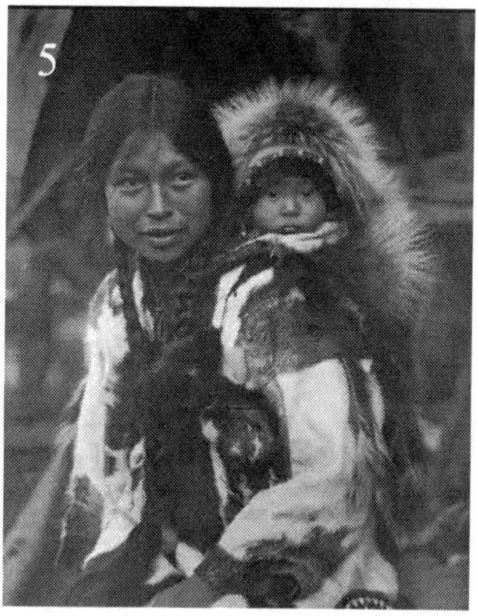
5

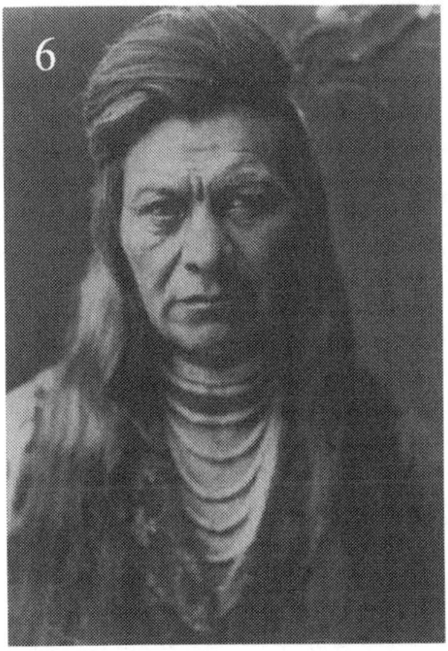
6

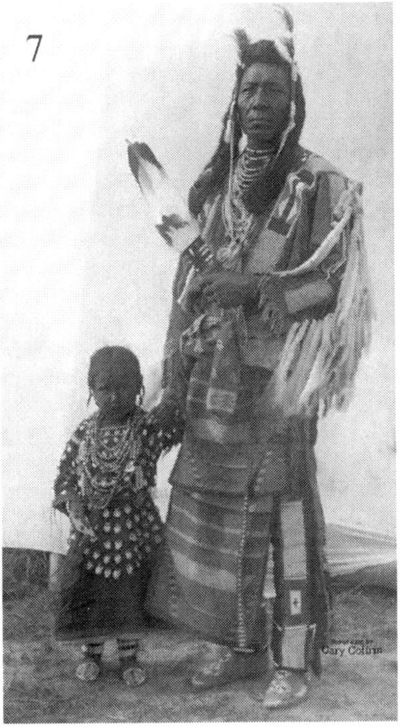
7

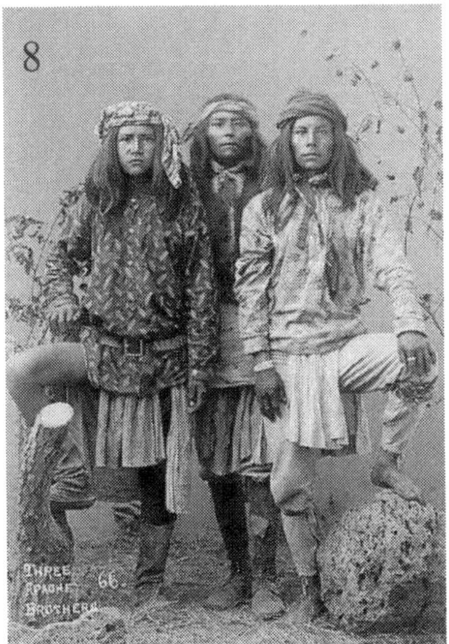
8
THREE
APACHE
BROTHERS
66.

104

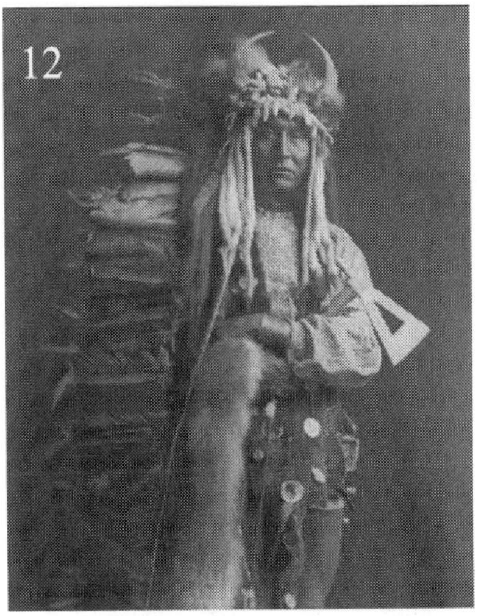
12

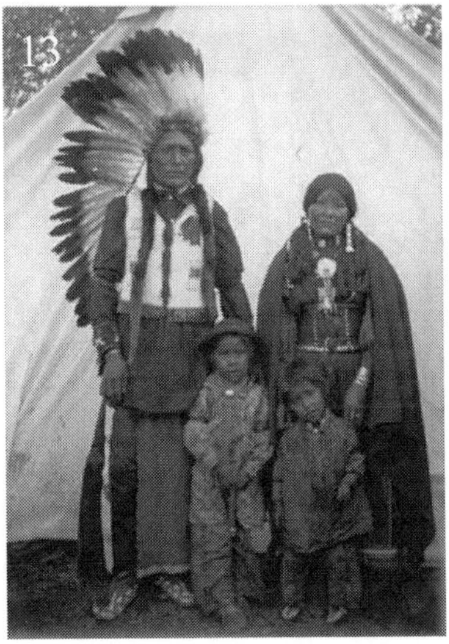
13

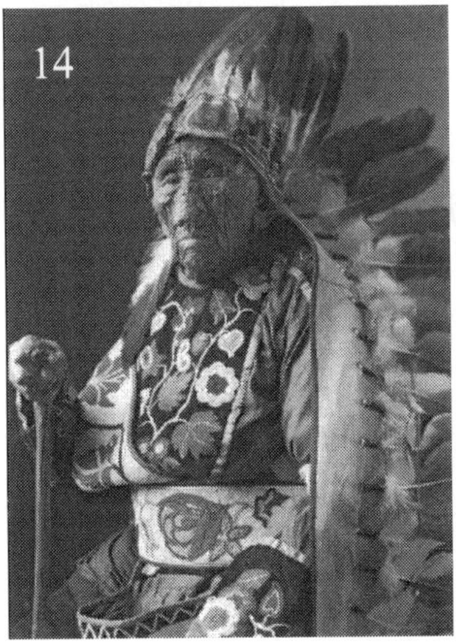
14

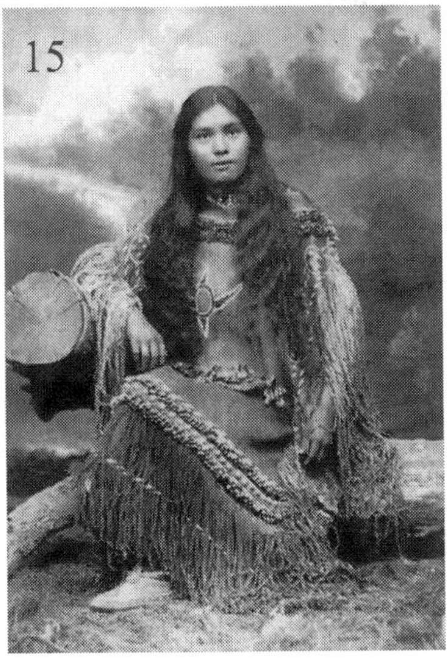
15

106

107

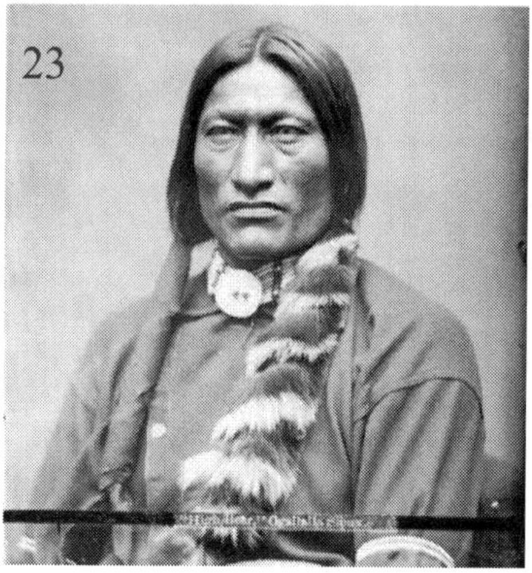
23

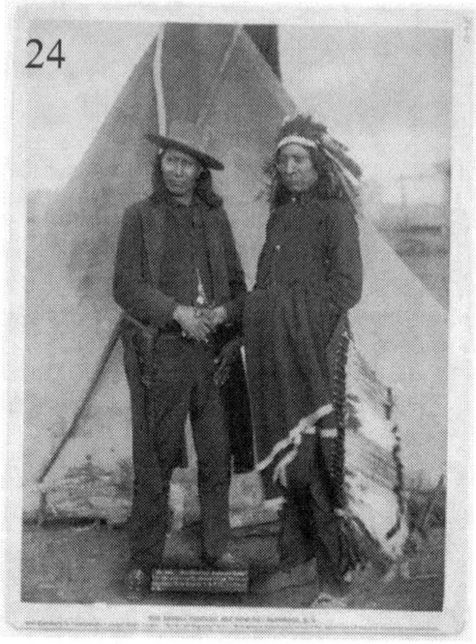
24

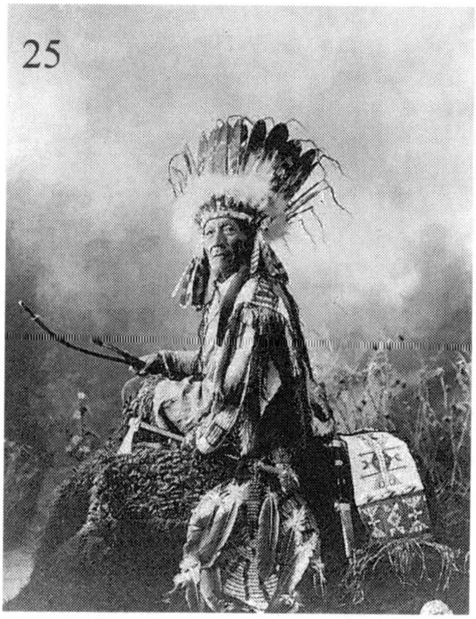
25

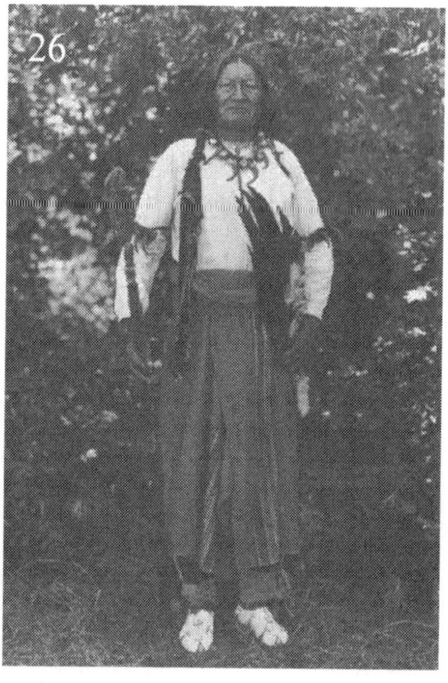
26

27

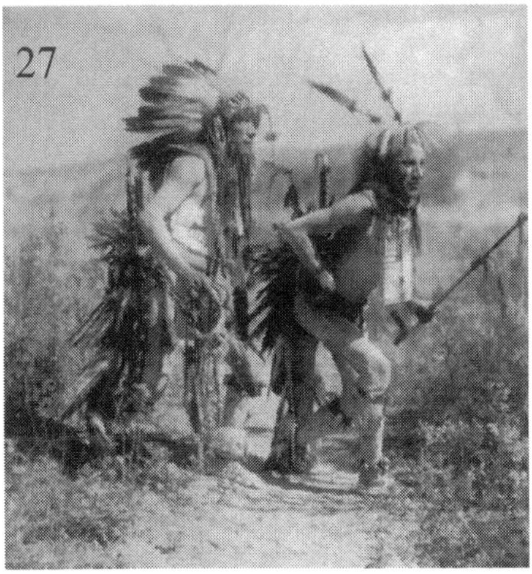

28

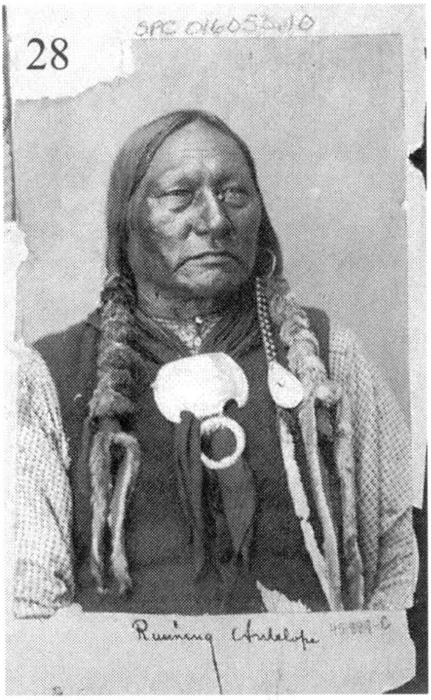

29

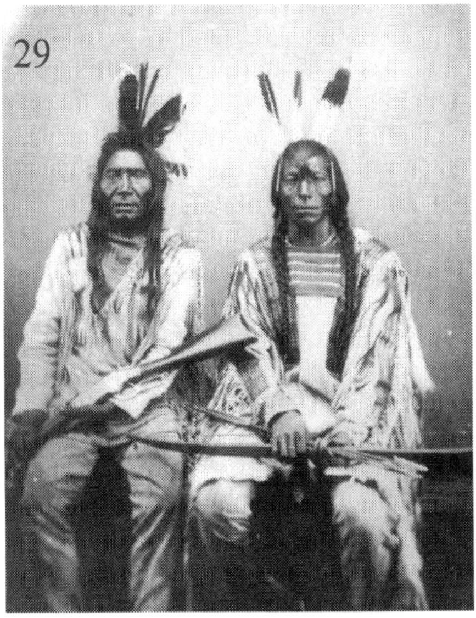

30

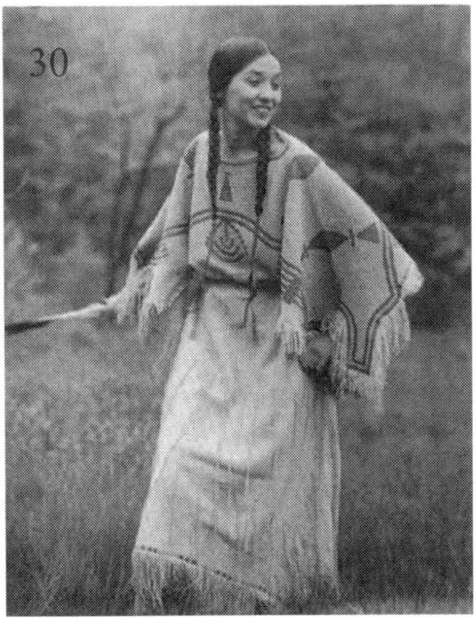

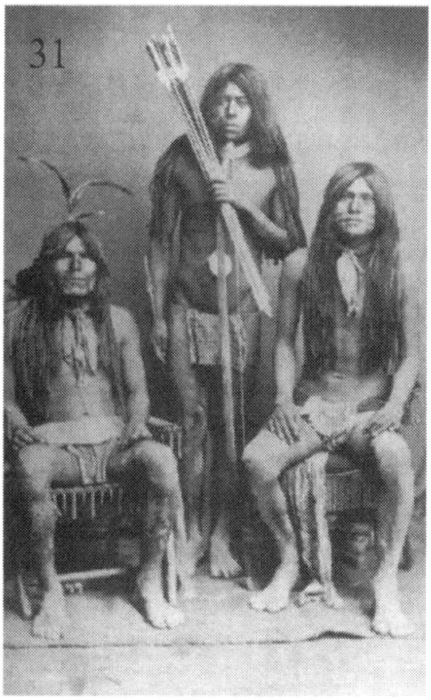
31

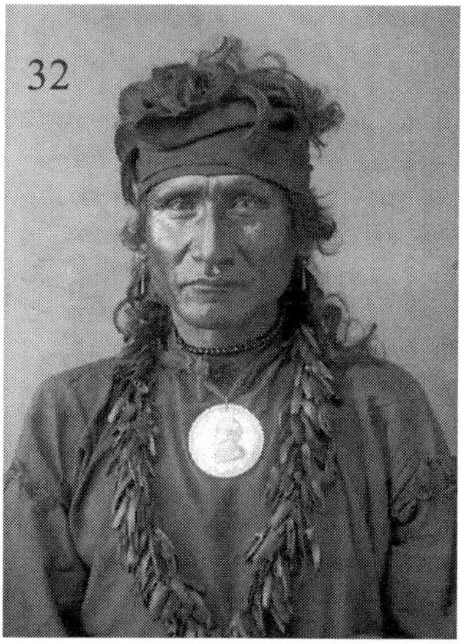
32

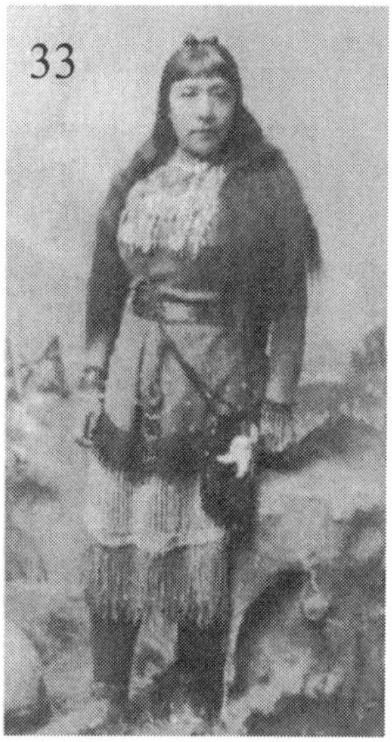
33

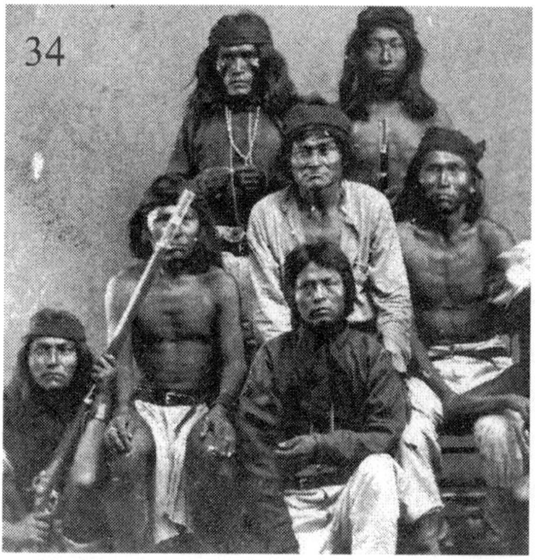
34

35

36

37

38

39

40

41

42

43

44

45

46

47

48

49

50

51

52

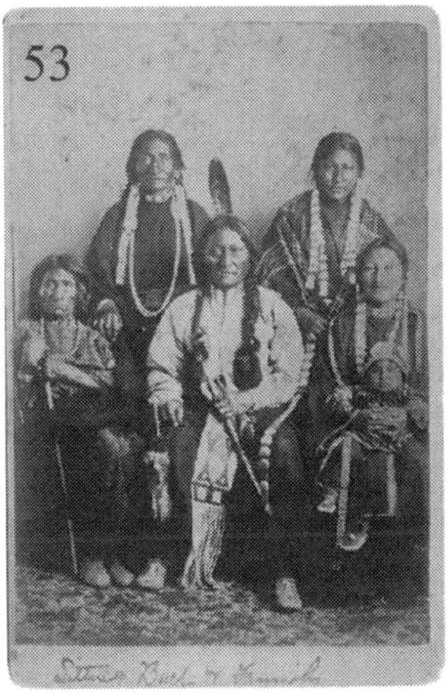
53

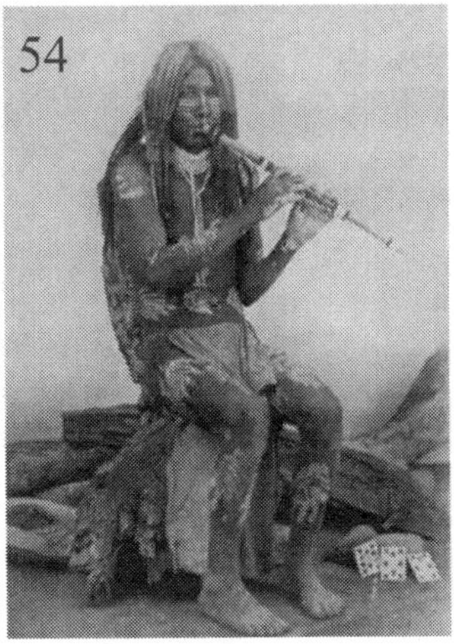
54

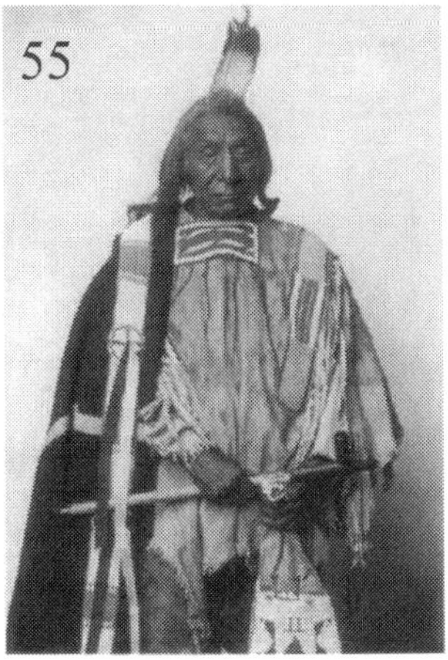
55

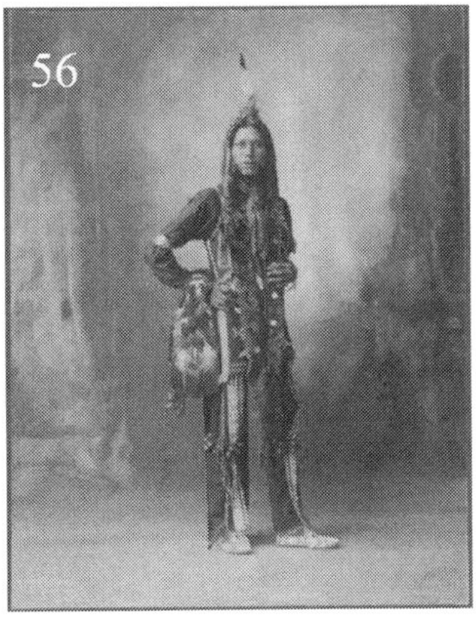
56

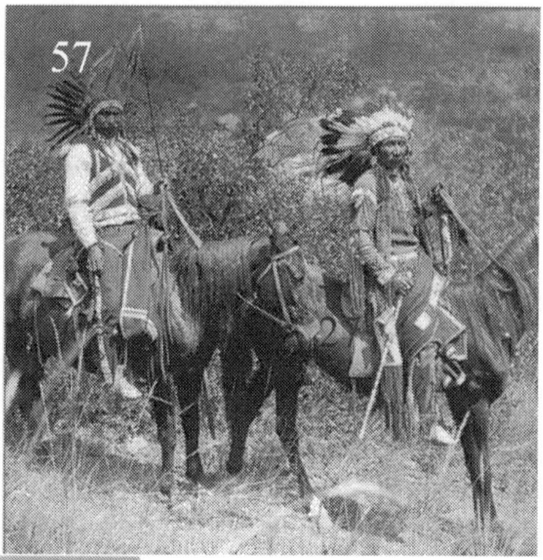
57

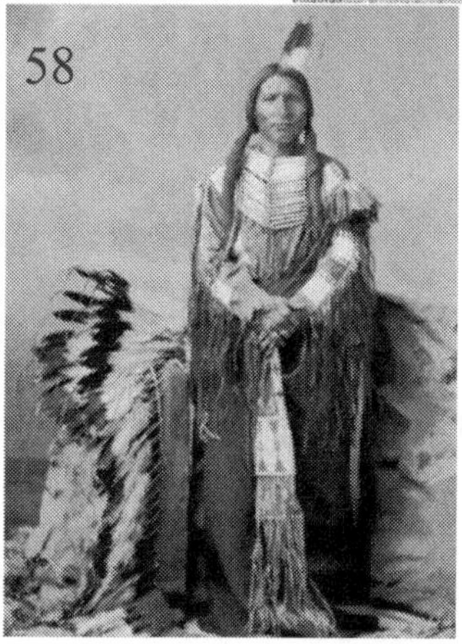
58

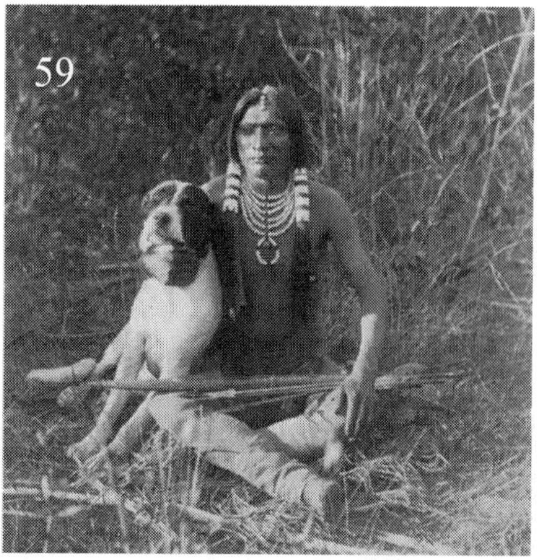
59

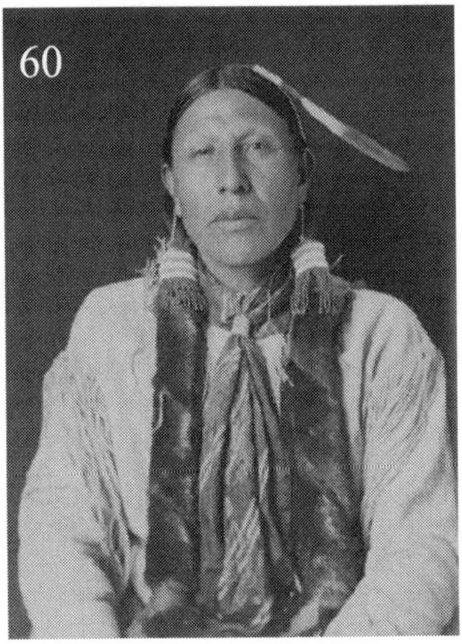

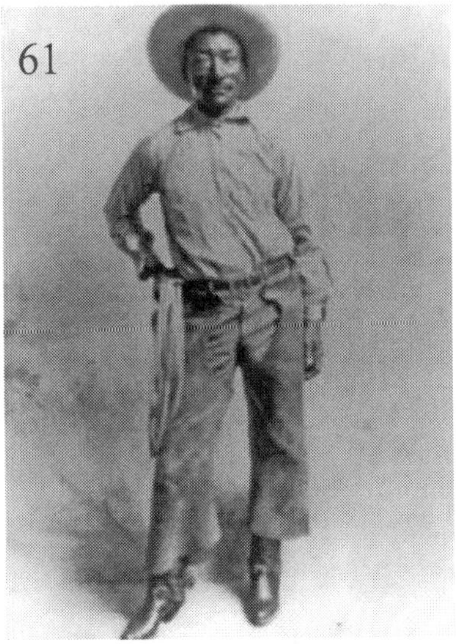

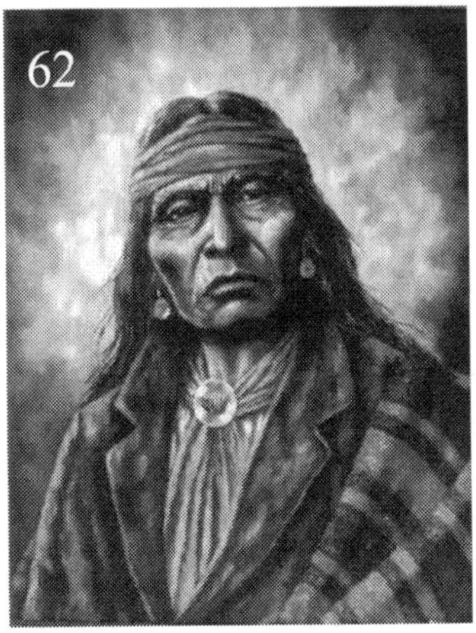

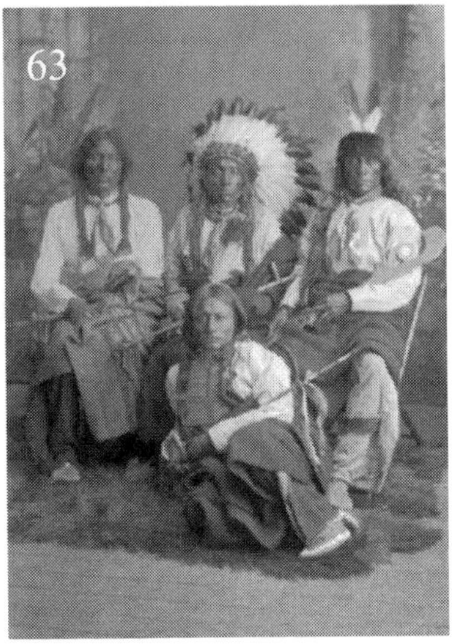

64

65

66

67

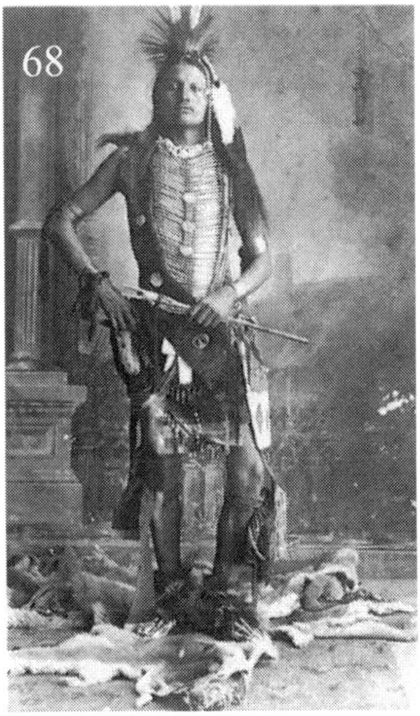
68

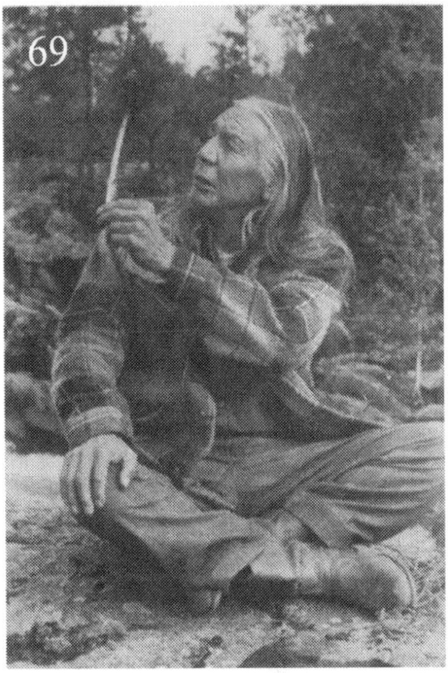
69

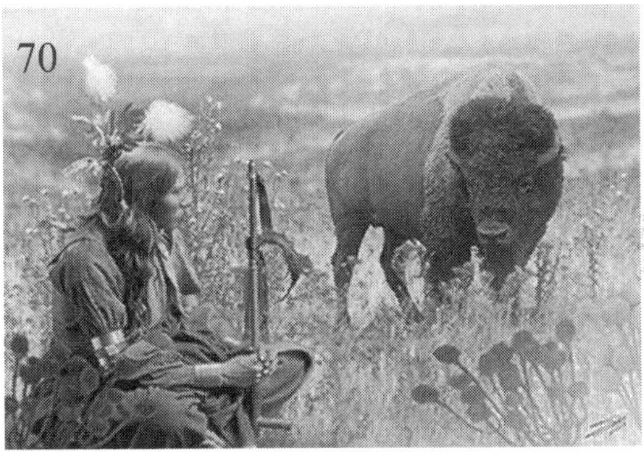
70

122

123

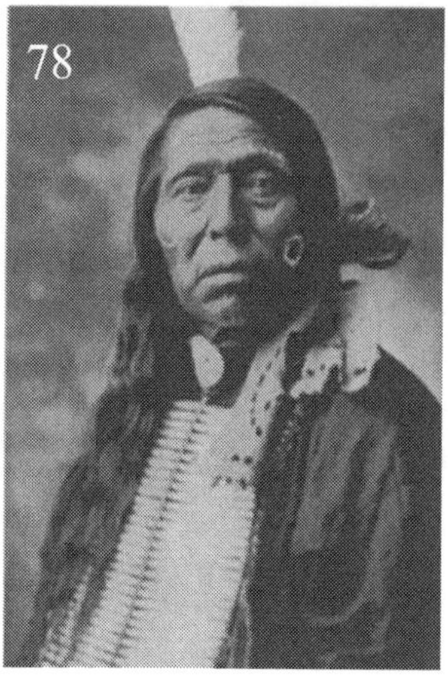
78

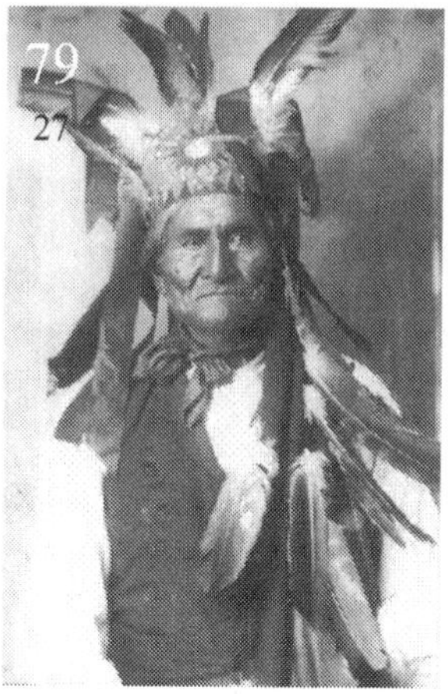
79
27

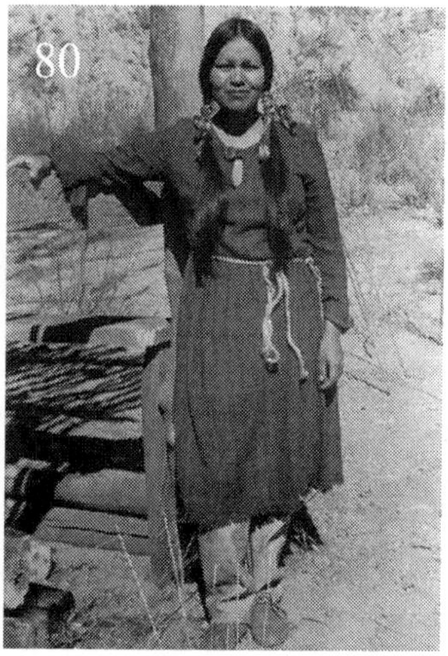
80

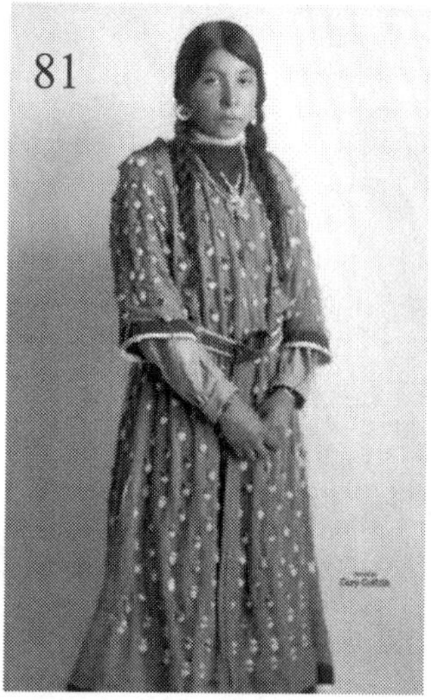
81

125

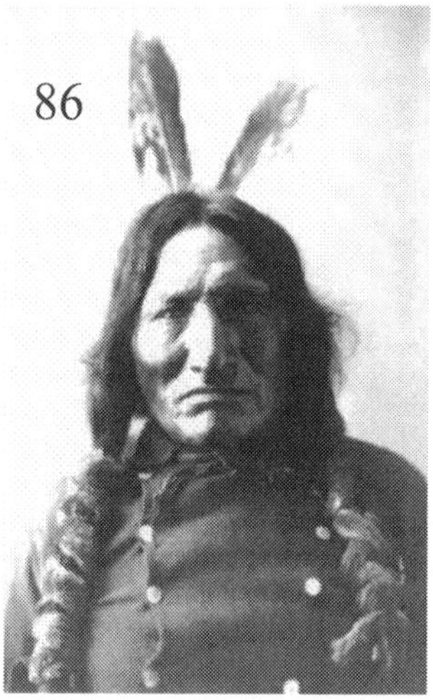
86

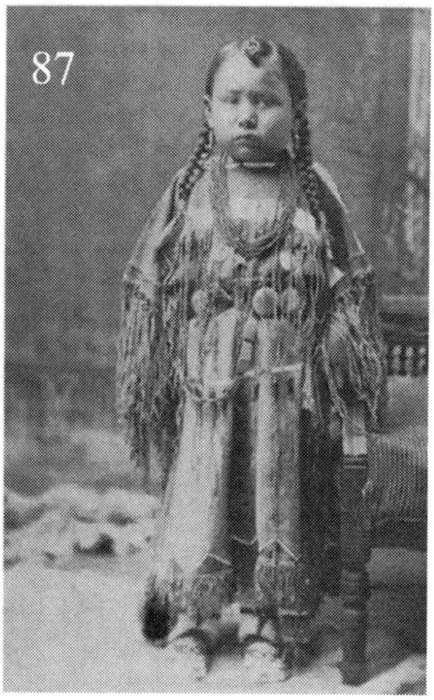
87

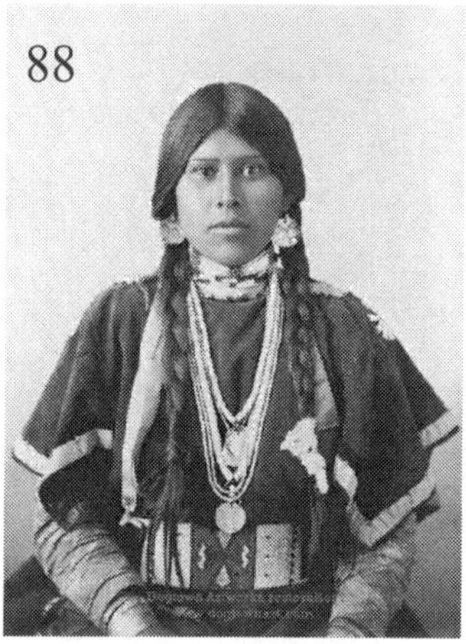
88

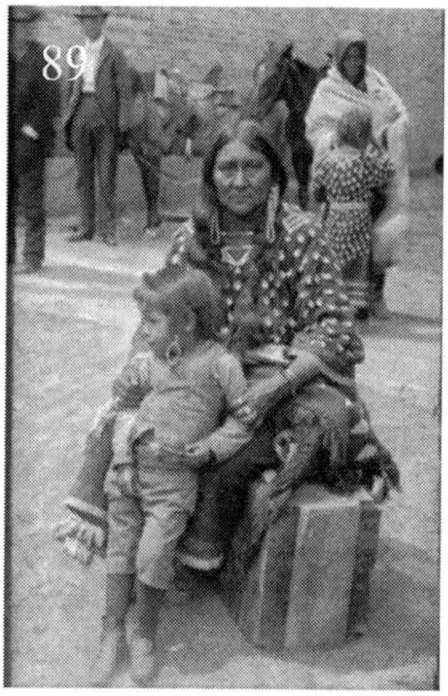
89

90

91

92

93

127

94

95

96

97

98

99

100

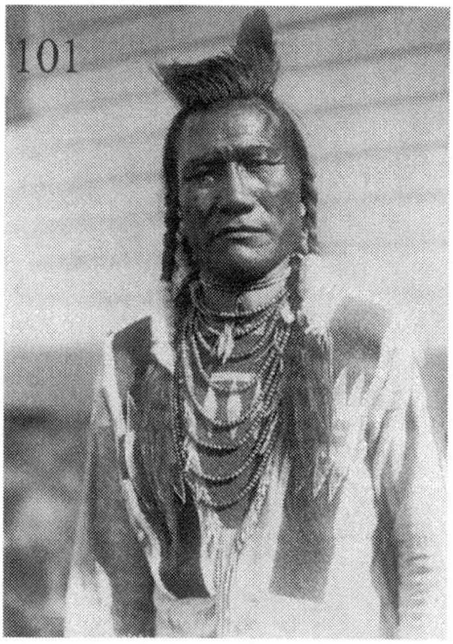

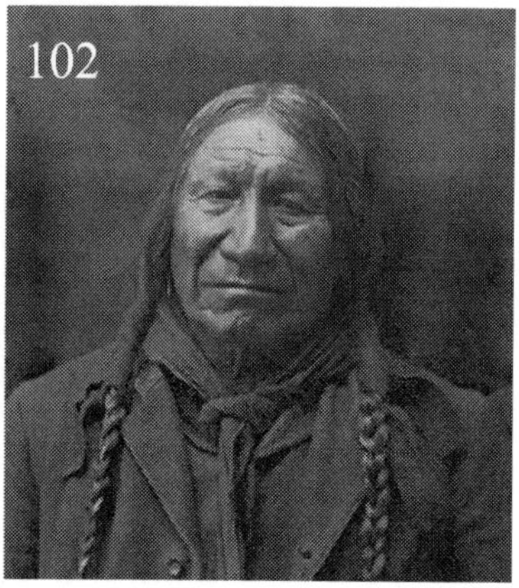

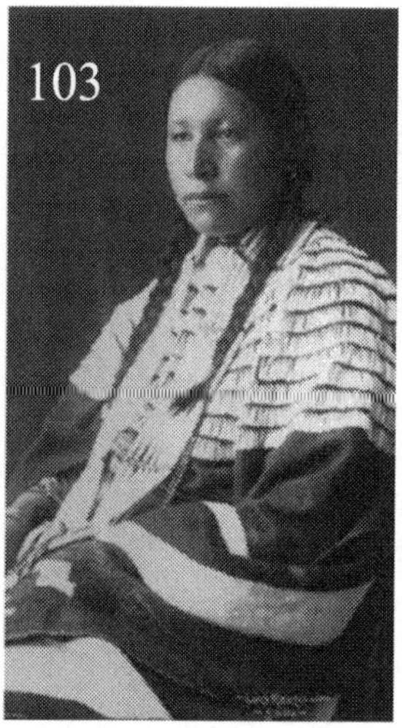

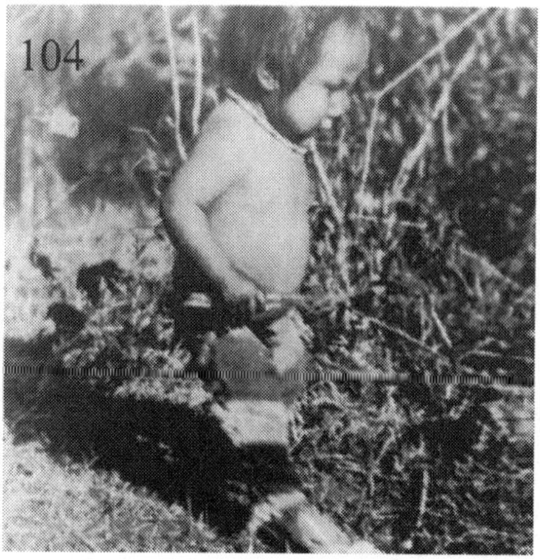

131

132

113

114

115

About the Author

Eleyes Y. Reeves was born in Indianapolis Indiana June 26 in the Lockfield Gardens Apartments. She is a Writer, Poet & Playwright and a Professional Portrait Artist. She went to Herron School of Art/IUPUI and received a Bachelors of Fine Arts Degree in Visual Communications 1982, at Herron School of Art/IUPUI, 1979 and a Bachelors of Art Degree in Psychology, Indiana University at Indianapolis. She is one of sixteen children her mother was Betty Jean Holiday Reeves and her father was Richard Alaska Reeves Sr. She started her own business in 1987 Eleyes Designs, and The 703 Gallery For The Arts, Inc. Suite at the Fall Creek building and a gift shop at 52nd & College, Georgia Peach Art Gift Shop and she is listed as Who's Who in the Outstanding Black Minority Women of Indiana

Books written by Eleyes Reeves: "Chillrens Are Peoples, Too!", "The Black
Panther Party Women", "Killin' of Sordid Gain", "Coonin'", Ona Oney Judge Staines The Slaves Who Knew They Could Fly With Jesus Christ" and "Aunt Ola: African American People & Native American Indian Tribes."

Calendars made: The Black Lives Mater World Murals Calendar, Eagle Wings (Sacred Prayer Calendar), The HOOD Calendar, The Ghetto Queen Calendar, & The American Black Graffiti Calendar

Plays written: "Tobin The Love Story", "Dido.Com The Time Traveler," "The Den", "Dido.Com & The Dragonslayers", and "O Susanna The Black Opera."

She was a grant writer from 1979-2019 for: Kwanzaa Fest presentations 1996-2000, Kwanzaa Fest (a city-wide festival), The Hidden Artists Exploratory Programs 1992-1996 sponsored by Lilly Endowment Inc., Federal Grant, NAG , UPS grant Emmis Community Relations, Campaign for Human Development grant, St. Rita Catholic Church Bowman-Francis Ministry, Society of the Divine Word (International & National), Neighborhood Association, Community Block Grants, Ruth Lilly Charitable Trust Fund and she also wrote several grants for MartindaleBrightwood Neighborhood Association.

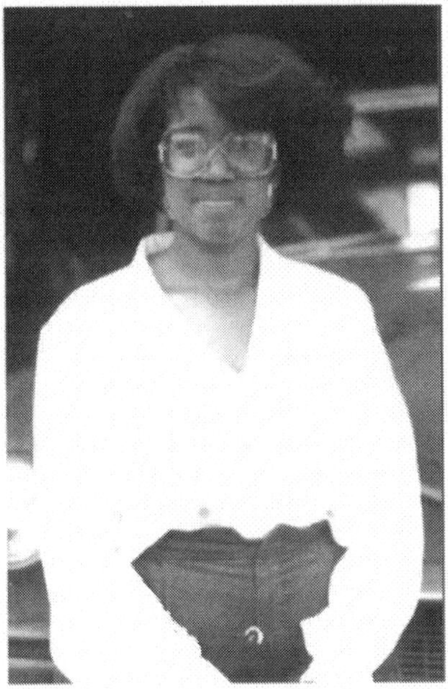

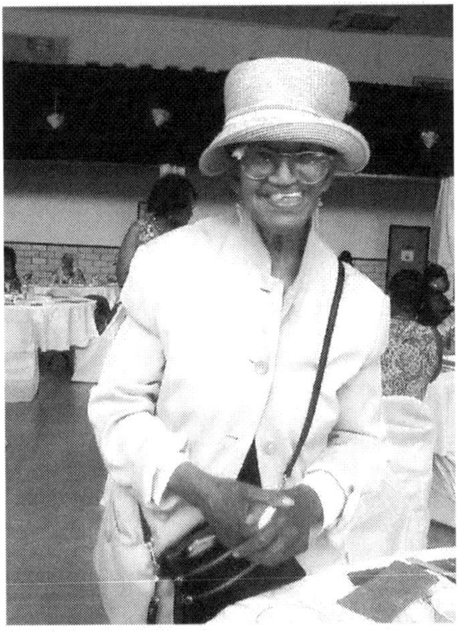

Made in the USA
Middletown, DE
16 August 2024